THE SOCIAL PROTECTION INDICATOR FOR THE PACIFIC

TRACKING DEVELOPMENTS IN SOCIAL PROTECTION

DECEMBER 2022

ASIAN DEVELOPMENT BANK

ADB

Contents

Tables, Figures, and Boxes

Tables

Figures

Foreword

Robust social protection systems are essential to fostering more inclusive and sustainable growth across Asia and the Pacific. In the Pacific island countries, where exposure and vulnerability to external shocks are among the highest in the world, social protection systems are all the more critical for strengthening community resilience and enabling individuals to thrive.

The Asian Development Bank (ADB) recognizes the central role of social protection in preparing for and responding to shocks, and emphasizes social protection systems as a key vehicle for achieving its strategic priority of addressing remaining poverty and reducing inequalities. Recognizing the need for evidence-based planning, ADB and its partners developed the Social Protection Indicator (SPI) as the first comprehensive and quantitative measure of social protection systems in Asia and the Pacific.

This report describes the SPI for ADB's 14 Pacific developing member countries (DMCs), calculated for 2018. It uses the SPI measure to assess the level of resources invested in social protection, as well as the value of benefits, coverage, and the distribution of expenditures in terms of poverty, gender, and disability. This report is the fourth in a series of Pacific regional SPI studies, published in 2012, 2016, and 2019. Building on the previous body of work, this report examines progress on social protection at the country and regional levels between 2009 and 2018, and captures the more recent lessons learned during the coronavirus (COVID-19) pandemic—all in support of fostering a more inclusive and resilient Pacific community.

The report advances several findings that can be used to underpin forward planning and implementation of social protection schemes across the region. Overall, the report considers how social protection in the Pacific can be made more inclusive, and how social protection can contribute to more resilient societies and economies in each of the Pacific DMCs. We hope that the SPI series continues to provide meaningful insights to governments and development partners in the region, and that the findings of this report will contribute to increasingly impactful social protection systems in each of the Pacific DMCs.

We thank everyone who contributed to this report, and we look forward to further engagement with social protection practitioners, advocates, and decision-makers across Asia and the Pacific in the years to come.

Leah Gutierrez
Director General
Pacific Department
Asian Development Bank

Bruno Carrasco
Director General concurrently Chief Compliance Officer
Sustainable Development and Climate Change Department
Asian Development Bank

Abbreviations

ADB	–	Asian Development Bank
COVID-19	–	coronavirus disease
CRPD	–	Convention on the Rights of Persons with Disabilities
CSO	–	civil society organization
DFAT	–	Department of Foreign Affairs and Trade, Government of Australia
DMC	–	developing member country
FSM	–	Federated States of Micronesia
GDP	–	gross domestic product
HDI	–	Human Development Index
HIES	–	household income and expenditure survey
LMP	–	labor market program
NGO	–	nongovernment organization
PNG	–	Papua New Guinea
SDG	–	Sustainable Development Goal
SPI	–	Social Protection Indicator
UNESCAP	–	United Nations Economic and Social Commission for Asia and the Pacific
UNICEF	–	United Nations Children's Fund
US	–	United States
WGQs	–	Washington Group questions
WHO	–	World Health Organization

Acknowledgments

This publication, *Social Protection Indicator for the Pacific: Tracking Developments in Social Protection*, is a collaboration between the Sustainable Development and Climate Change Department (SDCC) and the Pacific Department of the Asian Development Bank (ADB), led by Michiel Van der Auwera, former senior social development specialist, SDCC, and co-led by Ninebeth Carandang, principal social development specialist, Pacific Department, under the overall guidance of Wendy Walker, chief of the Social Development Thematic Group, SDCC.

The main chapters on the social protection indicator were written by Margaret Chung, ADB consultant for the Pacific report. This report contains special chapters on social protection for people with disabilities prepared by Joanna Rogers, ADB consultant on disability inclusion; on the socioeconomic impacts of and social protection responses to the coronavirus disease (COVID-19) written by Judy Otto, ADB consultant on the Pacific Islands; and a forward-looking chapter on the direction of social protection in the Pacific penned by Michael Samson, director at the Economic Policy and Research Institute. Flordeliza C. Huelgas, ADB consultant on social protection, provided technical guidance to review and consolidate data from 14 Pacific countries' calculations and reports prepared by national researchers Hillary Gorman (Cook Islands), Margaret Chung (Fiji), Johnny Hadley (Federated States of Micronesia), Teekoa Luta (Kiribati), Ramrakha Detenamo (Nauru), Vanessa Marsh (Niue), Judy Otto (Palau), Theodore Takpe (Papua New Guinea), Yolanda Elanzo (Marshall Islands), Sosefina Talauta-Tualaulelei (Samoa), Jaysie Boape (Solomon Islands), Joyce Mafi (Tonga), Filiga Nelu (Tuvalu), and Christy Haruel and Carol Dover (Vanuatu). These reports are available on request from ADB.

Special thanks to David Abbott, manager of data analysis and dissemination at the Statistics for Development Division of the Pacific Community, for providing guidance on country data collection and analysis. Babken Babajanian, ADB consultant, provided substantive inputs for finalizing the report.

The publication benefited from comments received from the Pacific Island countries' focal agencies and ADB's social protection technical working group.

Preparation of the report was supported by the Ireland Trust Fund for Building Climate Change and Disaster Resilience in Small Island Developing States.

Imelda Marquez provided administrative support. Kimberly Fullerton copyedited the manuscript, and Lumina Datamatics did the layout.

Executive Summary

This report presents the analysis of 2018 data on social protection programs in 14 Pacific developing member countries (DMCs) of the Asian Development Bank (ADB), namely, the Cook Islands, Fiji, Kiribati, the Marshall Islands, the Federated States of Micronesia (FSM), Nauru, Niue, Palau, Papua New Guinea (PNG), Samoa, Solomon Islands, Tonga, Tuvalu, and Vanuatu. Niue appears for the first time as a DMC. Timor-Leste, which was included in previous Pacific social protection reports is not included here as it is now being reflected as part of Southeast Asia.

The report uses the Social Protection Indicator (SPI) as its main measure for assessing social protection in the region. The SPI indicates the level of a DMC's resources invested in social protection, expressed as a percentage of gross domestic product (GDP) per capita. This report examines the nature and categories of social protection within and across the DMCs of the region, including the breadth of coverage; depth of benefits; and distribution of expenditure in regard to poverty, sex, and disability status. It examines changes in social protection between 2009 and 2018.

The SPI study gathered data on people with disabilities benefiting from social protection policy measures and programs for the first time. The report also presents the social protection response to the coronavirus disease (COVID-19) pandemic and discusses the future of social protection in the region.

The analysis in this report is derived from a series of national reports compiled by in-country consultants during 2020 and 2021 and draws on official information on government expenditures as well as administrative records on the number of social protection program beneficiaries. The report updates the 2015 ADB analysis *The Social Protection Indicator for the Pacific: Assessing Progress*.

Social protection expenditure in the Pacific is rising, but at modest rates

Overall expenditure on social protection in 14 Pacific DMCs in 2018 averages 5.5% of per capita GDP, a figure that ranged from 11.1% in Kiribati and 10.3% in the Marshall Islands to 1.5% in Tonga and 0.8% in Papua New Guinea (PNG). On average across eight countries with comparable data—Fiji, the Marshall Islands, Nauru, Palau, PNG, Samoa, Solomon Islands, and Vanuatu—the SPI steadily increased between 2009 (the first year it was measured) and 2018 (the reference year for this report), rising from 3.1% to 4.7% of per capita GDP. The steepest rise occurred between 2012 and 2015.

However, while the SPI values rose in these DMCs they tended to increase at a slower rate than the increases in nominal GDP, especially in those DMCs benefiting from fish license revenues. Social protection expenditure in current prices grew in several DMCs between 2015 and 2018, but so, too, did the GDPs of some DMCs.

Our analysis did not find a clear or consistent link between the level of SPI in the Pacific DMCs and country income, expressed in the World Bank's income categories of gross national income per capita. More influential factors appear to be either country-specific programs (e.g., the labor market program [LMP] in Kiribati that provides income-for-work in the copra sector) or a country's access to or links with social protection programs in the developed countries to which the country has an association (e.g., Niue's links to New Zealand, or the Marshall Islands and Palau's links to the United States).

Social insurance is the dominant social protection instrument

Social insurance is the first social protection category and refers to contributory schemes to cushion the risk associated with old age, health, disability, unemployment, and other events. Social insurance, namely pensions, have long dominated spending on social protection in the region. These are programs that usually provide retirement benefits to people at age 60 years, mainly covering those in formal employment or sometimes only public sector workers. Per capita returns from these programs are high and accrue to a small population group.

In 2018, the social insurance SPI accounts for a regional average of 2.9% of per capita GDP across 14 countries. Again, this figure varies across the region, ranging from 9.2% in Palau and 8.3% in the Marshall Islands to 0.5% in the Cook Islands and 0.1% in Nauru.

Based on comparable data from eight countries, social insurance has remained the largest component in each of the four SPI rounds between 2009 and 2018. In 2009, social insurance represented 2.4 percentage points (or 77.4%) of the aggregate SPI expenditure of 3.1% of GDP per capita. Social insurance contributed 2.8 percentage points (also equivalent to 77.4%) of the aggregate SPI of 3.3% of GDP per capita in 2012. The share of social insurance was equivalent to 3.3 percentage points (75.0%) of the SPI of 4.4% of GDP per capita in 2015, and to 3.4 percentage points (72.3%) of the SPI of 4.7% of GDP per capita in 2018.

The level of social insurance in total social protection expenditure has increased in terms of GDP per capita; however, the proportion of social protection expenditure going to social insurance has decreased slightly due to a larger proportion of expenditure going toward a more diverse pool of social assistance programs.

Health insurance is limited

Expenditures on other forms of social insurance, such as health insurance, are limited by comparison with pensions. Contributory health insurance programs are becoming more common, some operated by private companies and catering to people who can afford the premiums—mostly those in formal employment. They include, for example, Nambawan Super Limited and NasFund in PNG.

Other programs combine public and private investments. Thus, the two health insurance schemes in Palau are funded through mandatory contributions of 2.5% of earned incomes and government subsidized contributions for citizens who are over age 60 years and not working, and for people with disabilities who are not working. Together they cover almost the whole population of the country.

The lack of universal health insurance in most Pacific DMCs has been addressed through the provision of free or low-cost public health services. In Samoa, for example, the national health assistance program accounts for a significant part of social assistance. These services, however, provide for health care and do not compensate for the full consequences of ill health, such as loss of employment or death of a breadwinner.

Social assistance programs are expanding and becoming more diverse

Social assistance is the second social protection category and it refers to publicly funded cash and in-kind transfers and services, such as welfare payments, social pensions, and other support for vulnerable groups. The social assistance SPI across 14 countries averages 2.0% of GDP per capita in 2018. Values range across Pacific DMCs, from 7.0% in Tuvalu and 6.7% in Niue to virtually zero in PNG and Solomon Islands.

The rise in the SPI of the Pacific region was accompanied with a small, but significant, redirection of social protection expenditure toward social assistance. As a regional average, the SPI for social assistance rose from 0.6% of GDP per capita in 2009 to 1.2% in 2018. This reflects the increasing monetary value of individual benefits and greater investment in a larger number and greater range of social assistance programs. While expenditure under this category of programs is still much smaller than social insurance, it has seen the most growth since 2009.

A wider array of social assistance programs allows direct support toward addressing certain vulnerabilities in the region. Several DMCs have implemented universal assistance programs for vulnerable groups such as children, older people, and people with disabilities, moving away from the tightly means-tested and heavily administrated benefit systems once typical of the region.

Labor market programs remain modest

LMPs represent the third category of social protection and include programs that facilitate employment and promote efficient operation of labor markets, such as skills development and training, and public works—cash and food for work—programs. Active LMPs remain relatively underfunded and underdeveloped and remain a mere fraction of the size of the other two social protection categories.

Expenditure is smallest on active LMPs, averaging only 0.6% of per capita GDP across the region in 2018. These programs aim to increase access to paid employment and are mostly targeted at the unemployed and people yet to enter the work force. Expenditure on active LMPs in Fiji, the Marshall Islands, Nauru, Palau, PNG, Samoa, Solomon Islands, and Vanuatu increased from a regional average of 0.1% of per capita GDP in 2009 to 0.2% in both 2015 and 2018. Active LMPs are receiving more attention due to the COVID-19 pandemic, presenting an opportunity for supporting their expansion.

Coverage has widened but large gaps remain

Social protection program coverage levels are low or very low in most Pacific DMCs. Social protection in 14 Pacific countries covered 32.0% of intended beneficiaries in 2018, leaving a substantial share of eligible persons without support.

Of the three categories, social assistance has the widest breadth of coverage or the proportion of intended beneficiaries covered by the program at 20.6%. Social insurance has a narrow coverage of 9.9%. The regional average coverage for social insurance is pulled up by Palau's high figure. Leaving Palau out of the calculation, the regional average drops to 2.6%, a more realistic indicator of the narrow coverage of social insurance programs—mainly provident funds—in most Pacific DMCs. LMPs have the most restricted breadth of coverage of only 4.6%.

The breadth of social protection coverage widened between 2009 and 2018, from 14.9% to 40.2% in aggregate across all DMCs. Palau had the greatest increase, mostly due to expanded social insurance programs, and in Fiji and Nauru, increases in breadth of coverage reflected new social assistance programs.

Benefits tend to be small and narrowly distributed

The depth of benefits—the average value of the benefits received by each actual beneficiary as a share of GDP per capita—is greatest for social insurance, averaging 103.7% of GDP per capita in 2018. However, relatively large benefit amounts go to small groups of people as monthly pensions or lump-sum retirement payments due to narrow coverage of social insurance programs.

Benefits from social assistance programs are considerably smaller, at an average of 15.4% of per capita GDP in 2018. Average benefits from LMPs are larger, at 27.3% of GDP per capita, but the pool of beneficiaries is very small. Again, there is wide variation in these values across DMCs.

The SPI analysis suggests that where coverage is high, average social protection benefits tend to be relatively small, as in the Cook Islands, Fiji, the Marshall Islands, Nauru, Palau, and Vanuatu. The opposite situation also holds—where average benefits are relatively large, coverage is generally low, as in Kiribati, the Federated States of Micronesia (FSM), PNG, Solomon Islands, and Tuvalu.

The depth of benefits of social protection programs changed over between 2009 and 2018, but not in a uniform manner. The Marshall Islands, Samoa, and Solomon Islands saw gains in depth. In both Solomon Islands and Samoa, this reflects greater per capita benefits from social assistance programs, and in Solomon Islands alone, also from active LMPs. The depth of social protection programs decreased in Nauru, Vanuatu, Palau, Fiji, and, most notably, PNG. In most DMCs, this situation demonstrates a larger range of social assistance programs with more widely distributed benefits.

Social protection favors the nonpoor, but spending on the poor is increasing

Social protection spending in the Pacific continues to favor the nonpoor over the poor. In 2018, the SPI for the nonpoor is greater than the SPI for the poor in most countries, except in Kiribati, reflecting its investment in supporting informal sector producers.

This situation has changed little from 2015 and earlier. In 2018, social protection expenditure received by the poor averages 1.2% of GDP per capita, while the nonpoor received 3.6% of GDP per capita, little change from 1.0% and 3.4%, respectively, in 2015.

This is largely because of the large amount of social insurance expenditure that principally benefits formal sector workers, often the population with more secure and better-paid employment.

Between 2009 and 2018, the share of social protection benefits going to the poor grew in seven of eight countries with comparable data—Nauru, PNG, Palau, the Marshall Islands, Samoa, Solomon Islands and Vanuatu. The share of social protection benefits going to the poor decreased in Fiji, as it expanded some universal social assistance programs.

Social protection spending is more favorable for men, but gender gap has narrowed in some countries

Social protection spending in the Pacific continued to favor men over women in 2018, continuing the earlier trend, with social protection programs spending, on average, 2.5% of GDP per capita on men and 2.2% on women, figures barely changed from 2015. Social protection expenditure in 2018 is more favorable for women in Nauru and quite equal in Palau, the Cook Islands, and Samoa, but spending for men outstrips that for women in Fiji, Kiribati, PNG, Solomon Islands, and Vanuatu.

The gender gap is widest in social insurance, mainly due to higher expenditure on superannuation and other insurance programs that disproportionately benefit men. This reflects the greater proportion of men in formal employment, their generally higher rates of pay, and thereby their greater opportunity to benefit from superannuation and other contributory insurance programs.

Seven of eight countries with comparable data—Nauru, PNG, Palau, the Marshall Islands, Samoa, Solomon Islands, and Vanuatu—increased their spending for women between 2009 and 2018.

Since 2015, the difference between social protection expenditure for women and for men has narrowed in the Marshall Islands, the FSM, Nauru, Palau, Samoa, and Solomon Islands; widened in the Cook Islands, Tonga, and Vanuatu; and showed little appreciable change in Fiji, Kiribati, and PNG. Where the gap narrowed, it mostly reflects greater access to social assistance programs, especially for older people, as women dominate this age group because of their greater average longevity.

Social protection in the Pacific needs to be more disability inclusive

The regional average SPI in 2018 for people living with disabilities was 0.5%, lower than the regional average of 5.0% for those without disabilities. The SPI data suggest that the proportion of social protection expenditure reaching people with disabilities could be almost zero in some DMCs when only disability-targeted programs are considered. It is, however, likely that people with disabilities benefit—to some extent—from general social protection programs, such as noncontributory old-age pensions and health assistance.

The 2006 Commission for the Rights of Persons with Disability (CRPD) and 2012 Incheon Strategy, together with the Pacific Framework for the Rights of Persons with Disabilities, 2016–2025, set out a subregional agenda for disability-inclusive social protection. This is increasingly reflected in social protection policies and programs to address the needs of people with disabilities. Seven of the 14 Pacific DMCs—the Cook Islands, Fiji, Kiribati, Nauru, Niue, Palau, and Tuvalu—have social assistance programs; the adequacy and coverage, however, require further study.

Pacific DMCs have paid more attention to disability-inclusive social protection since ratifying the CRPD, but more needs to be done. Disability-inclusive social protection should combine access to general social protection programs and additional disability benefits that address the extra costs of disability. Social services and access to assistive devices and technology, rehabilitation programs, and employment and/or education programs also form a part of disability-inclusive social protection. Better understanding is needed of how these programs and measures overlap to build knowledge about social protection coverage and the amount of support that people with disabilities can access.

The coronavirus disease crisis prompted many developing member countries to enhance social protection measures

The 14 Pacific DMCs were quick to respond to COVID-19 by declaring states of emergency, drawing up COVID-19 contingency plans, implementing health protocols, closing borders in 2020, and by undertaking mass vaccination campaigns. Combined, these measures were largely successful in keeping the virus at bay, albeit at significant economic and social costs.

Countries in the region employed existing social protection mechanisms and established new mechanisms to mitigate some of the worst impacts of the COVID-19 pandemic, including the following:

- social insurance mechanisms to address unemployment arising from COVID-19, including direct cash payments, disbursement from retirement fund savings, lines of credit, and cash-for-work schemes;
- social assistance mechanisms to assist the most vulnerable, including conditional and unconditional cash transfers, utility subsidies, in-kind food distribution, sick leave;
- innovative wage and training subsidies paid directly to employers to incentivize their retention of employees while using "down-time" to upskill their workforce in preparation for reopening of borders; and
- measures to support the private sector to withstand the economic downturn, such as grants or loans to businesses, training for informal and microenterprise entrepreneurs, subsidies for state-owned enterprises and cash crop producers, waivers of taxes and fees, and various forms of repayment holidays for businesses unable to keep pace with loan repayments.

The COVID-19 crisis has heightened awareness of the need for formal, government-supported social protection systems, operating in tandem with the traditional "sharing and caring" that takes place at community and family levels. DMCs that had a systematic approach to social protection pre-COVID were able to respond faster and more efficiently than those with piecemeal systems. This lesson is being taken to heart by several DMCs. Thus, Fiji, Nauru, and PNG are taking the lead, together with the World Bank and ADB, to apply the lessons of the COVID-19 period toward design of new national social protection policies.

Future directions for social protection in the Pacific

The past decade has seen governments across the Pacific recognize the potential of social protection instruments to reinforce community-based mechanisms for tackling hardship, vulnerability, and risk, particularly in the face of increasingly severe natural, epidemiological, and economic shocks. Five trends will likely shape the future of social protection in this region:

(i)   Pacific DMCs are expanding social pensions, disability grants, child benefits, and other programs that increasingly cover an expanding share of the population. Integrated COVID-19 recovery strategies and the development of more shock-responsive and adaptive systems in the face of future shocks will reinforce this trend.

(ii)   Governments are focusing on child-sensitive social protection investments in early childhood development, building the foundation for human and cognitive capital that drives future prosperity. The region's rising demographic dependency ratios will continue to drive the demand for these investments, reinforced by COVID-19's changes in work norms and technologies that elevate the associated returns to human and cognitive capital.

(iii) Pacific DMCs stand to benefit from social protection initiatives that strengthen livelihoods and employment, particularly for youth who face the highest unemployment rates of any working-age demographic. The priority of creating youth opportunities, intensified by the risks of future crises, will accelerate these regional and national youth development initiatives that support intergenerational social contracts that reap demographic dividends and sustain life-cycle social protection systems.

(iv)   Governments and their development partners are integrating opportunities for inclusive digital technologies both into their social protection systems and their larger development frameworks, with spillover benefits that strengthen linkages to telehealth, remote education, e-markets, adaptive livelihoods, financial inclusion, systems-driven social protection, and other developmental areas. These patterns, trends, and opportunities interact to strengthen the knowledge-based economic sectors, aligning the priorities of crisis response and recovery with the major economic growth opportunities of the 21st century.

(v)   The COVID-19 pandemic—both with its devastating economic impacts as well as its foreshadowing of future crises—has accelerated Pacific DMCs' embrace of national social protection policies, strategies, and frameworks. These initiatives consolidate collaborative approaches, strengthen opportunities for policy expansion, and better enable integrated and comprehensive social protection systems to optimize a mix of climate and development strategies.

I. Overview and Methodology

The Social Protection Indicator for Pacific Developing Member Countries

This report describes the Social Protection Indicator (SPI) for Pacific developing member countries (DMCs) calculated for 2018. It is the fourth in a series of regional Pacific SPI reports; other reports were based on data from 2009, 2012, and 2015, and published in 2012, 2016, and 2019, respectively.[1] Intended to systematically track and to assess developments in social protection, these reports built upon national SPI reports compiled during the same years.

The analysis in this report covers 14 Pacific countries, including the Cook Islands, Fiji, Kiribati, the Marshall Islands, the Federated States of Micronesia (FSM), Nauru, Niue, Palau, Papua New Guinea (PNG), Samoa, Solomon Islands, Tonga, Tuvalu, and Vanuatu. Niue appears for the first time as a DMC. Timor-Leste, which was included in previous social protection reports, is not included here.

Social protection is defined as a set of policies and programs designed to reduce poverty and vulnerability by promoting efficient labor markets, diminishing people's exposure to risks, and enhancing their capacity to protect themselves against hazards and/or interruption and/or loss of income.[2] These programs fall into three broad categories: social insurance, social assistance, and labor market programs (LMPs).

Social insurance programs include contributory pensions; health insurance; and other insurance schemes such as provident funds, unemployment insurance, and worker compensation schemes. Social insurance programs are contributory and benefit mostly those employed in the civil service and well-established private companies.

Social assistance programs are noncontributory and directed toward people vulnerable to common types of risks, including children; older people; persons with disabilities; the poor; and those who face economic and social disadvantages associated with, for example, aging, sickness, poor access to education, and other basic services.

---

[1]   ADB. 2012. *The Revised Social Protection Index: Methodology and Handbook.* Manila; ADB. 2016. *The Social Protection Indicator: Assessing Results for the Pacific.* Manila; and ADB. 2019. *The Social Protection Indicator for the Pacific: Assessing Progress.* Manila.

[2]   ADB. 2003. *Social Protection—Our Framework: Policies and Strategies.* Manila.

Aimed mainly at unemployed and underemployed persons, LMPs include both active LMPs (e.g., food- or cash-for-work schemes) and passive LMPs (e.g., unemployment insurance, maternity leave, and disability insurance). The SPI categorizes passive LMPs under social insurance. The analysis of the SPI gender dimension draws on sex-disaggregated data.

The SPI shows government total expenditure on social protection expressed as a percentage of gross domestic product (GDP) per capita. An indicator developed by the Asian Development Bank (ADB), the SPI monitors and reports on the progress of social protection programs in its DMCs to gauge overall expenditure and coverage of these programs, thereby assessing their adequacy. As described below, the SPI is derived from official data on government expenditure and beneficiaries of social protection programs.[3]

The previous SPI report focusing on the Pacific, from 2015, found that the coverage of social protection programs in the region was improving but needed to be extended; social protection benefits were limited for most poor people, and social assistance programs did not adequately support the vulnerable; spending on social insurance dominated and mostly benefited a small number of formal sector workers; and active LMPs were especially underdeveloped.[4] The report recommended that assistance to children be expanded, overall social protection be made more gender-sensitive, and social protection policy frameworks be strengthened.

Based on the same methodology and data sources as the previous SPI reports, this report examines how SPIs have changed from 2015 to 2018, both in individual DMCs and in the Pacific region generally. In light of recent developments in the region, this report also focuses on persons with disabilities and the impact of the COVID-19 pandemic on each DMC.

Structure of the Report

Chapter I presents the SPI methodology and key findings of the analysis. Chapter II discusses overall social protection expenditure in 2018 as a share of aggregate GDP and of GDP per capita for each intended beneficiary; expenditure on each of the three categories of social protection and programs within these categories; as well as comparisons over time, since the first regional SPI report in 2009. Chapter III discusses the depth and breadth of social protection benefits; distributional dimensions of social protection relating to poverty, sex, and disability status; and patterns of change in the SPI since 2009.

For the first time, the SPI has added a disability dimension of social protection to assess the extent to which people with disabilities receive social protection support. Chapter IV examines how the special needs of people with disabilities are being addressed through existing social protection programs. Chapter V documents the social protection response to address the impact of the COVID-19 pandemic on the people

---

3   ADB. 2012. *The Revised Social Protection Index: Methodology and Handbook.* Manila.
4   ADB. 2019. *The Social Protection Indicator for the Pacific: Assessing Progress.* Manila.

and economies of this region. Chapter VI goes beyond the statistical analysis of the SPI to consider progress made by Pacific DMCs over the past decade toward expanding and improving social protection policies and programs. The appendix to the report includes detailed tables to support the SPI analysis.

Methodology

This report is based on official data and other information collected in each of ADB's 14 Pacific DMCs in 2020 and 2021. The 2011 methodology for data collection and analysis is followed.[5] The SPI is expressed in terms of a DMC's GDP per capita:

$$SPI = \frac{Social\ protection\ expenditure}{target\ beneficiaries} \div GDP\ per\ capita$$

An SPI value of 3.5%, for example, indicates that a DMC's social protection expenditure for targeted beneficiaries amounts to 3.5% of its GDP per capita. The SPI data also allow for analysis of benefit adequacy as well as the distribution of expenditure across all groups of intended beneficiaries as (i) depth of benefits, and (ii) breadth of coverage. The depth of benefits refers to the average expenditure per actual beneficiary as a percentage of GDP per capita. The breadth of coverage refers to the proportion of actual beneficiaries who receive social protection benefits relative to total target beneficiaries. Together, these measurements demonstrate broader patterns of equal—or unequal—distribution of benefits across a population. Although the SPI is a useful measure of social protection system performance, it is, however, only one measure. Other aspects not fully covered here include poverty impact and targeting efficiency.[6]

The intended beneficiaries of social protection expenditures vary by program and DMC, although there are many similarities given the detailed selection criteria outlined in Table 1. In some situations, coverage may exceed 100% of intended beneficiaries, indicating that some beneficiaries receive more than one kind of benefit. An older person, for example, may be eligible to receive a pension as well as health assistance benefits.

Consultants were engaged in each country to collect and to input the required data into spreadsheets constructed by ADB. Government statistics and reports are supplemented, when necessary, with other published data sources, reports by international finance institutions and bilateral agencies, and discussions and interviews with agencies responsible for social protection programs.[7]

---

[5] ADB. 2012. *The Revised Social Protection Index: Methodology and Handbook.* Manila.
[6] Aspects of methodology beyond the scope of this report are discussed in International Labour Organization (ILO). 2021. *World Social Protection Report, 2020–22: Social Protection at the Crossroads—In Pursuit of a Better Future.* Geneva; and World Bank. 2018. *The State of Social Safety Nets 2018.* Washington, DC.
[7] Social protection spending, coverage, and performance are measured globally in ILO. 2021. *World Social Protection Report, 2020–22: Social Protection at the Crossroads—In Pursuit of a Better Future.* Geneva; and World Bank. 2018. *The State of Social Safety Nets 2018.* Washington, DC.

Table 1: Intended Social Protection Beneficiary Groups

Program	Group
Social Insurance	
Health insurance	Employed population if it is contributory; if universal coverage, the total population is the reference population
Unemployment insurance	Employed population
Pensions	Population ages 60 years and over
Social Assistance	
Welfare assistance	Poor population (living below the nationally defined poverty line, all ages)
Child welfare	Children, ages 0–14 years
Health assistance	Poor population
Assistance to older people	Poor older persons
Disability assistance	Persons with disabilities
Labor market programs	
Skills development and training	Unemployed and underemployed
Cash- and food-for-work	Unemployed and underemployed

Source: ADB. 2012. *The Revised Social Protection Index: Methodology and Handbook*. Manila.

Data were collected in each country from mid-2020 to early 2021, at a time when many Pacific DMCs and government agencies were disrupted by COVID-19 pandemic shutdowns. In some DMCs, data collection still proceeded well, and consultants reported good cooperation with agencies. The pandemic situation, however, was partly responsible for the slow process of data collection in other DMCs. It was particularly difficult when the research had to be conducted remotely, as this contributed to poor response rates. Other difficulties include the consistency of the data and ability to make meaningful comparisons over periods of time. Some basic data were sourced from censuses, which DMCs generally conduct on 5- or 10-year cycles. Most poverty-related data, however, came from household income expenditure surveys (HIESs), which are conducted haphazardly, and their analyses and publications even more so. In Fiji, for example, the latest official publication of full HIES data dates from 2008–2009, as only preliminary findings have been released from the 2013–2014 HIES. Any later figures are only estimates.[8]

In addition, some agencies responsible for social protection programs had difficulty extracting data from their administrative records. Every government in the region has computerized record-keeping systems, yet some agencies reported that basic data are compiled manually or do not exist in any disaggregated manner. In most DMCs, social protection agencies have few staff members, are tasked with heavy workloads and responsibilities, and are constrained by inadequate program management information systems. Nonetheless, the data required for the SPI analysis principally involve the cost of programs and the number and basic characteristics of beneficiaries—information that is fundamental to the management of any such program.

---

[8] Government of Fiji, Fiji Bureau of Statistics. 2015. 2013–14 Household Income and Expenditure Survey Preliminary Findings: Release 1. In *Statistical News*. 31 December.

Although this SPI reporting process began a decade ago, agencies responsible for social protection policies and programs are just starting to recognize the value that the analysis can provide. More broadly, key staff members may not be cognizant of the value of their own administrative records in designing and assessing their policies and programs. This lack of awareness sometimes manifests through a misunderstanding of how administrative data can be used without jeopardizing privacy requirements. Over the past decade, there has been considerable investment in improving the use of administrative data in other sectors, principally health and education, which has helped improve the management of these services. Such investment in information management should be extended to assist social protection agencies, a much smaller—but equally important—undertaking. This also points to the need for stronger advocacy of the SPI indicator findings by the bank.

Since the endorsement of the Convention on the Rights of Persons with Disabilities (CRPD) by most Pacific island countries, many governments in the region have introduced various assistance programs for people with disabilities. Data exist on these programs, yet few agencies are able to report on the participation of people with disabilities in general social protection programs to which, of course, they may also be entitled. The picture that has emerged so far on social protection for people with disabilities is therefore incomplete. A key challenge in the region includes poor information management and insufficient agency cooperation (Box 1). Improving this understanding through the collection of disaggregated data is fundamental to refining services for them.

Box 1: Common Data Collection Difficulties for the Social Protection Indicator

Poor information management. One country Social Protection Indicator report noted that collecting data was challenging, particularly because social protection data are stored in Excel documents. To examine specific data sets, therefore, information must be manually collated. Sex-disaggregated data on beneficiaries are not regularly monitored and must be entered and collated manually. Disability-disaggregated data are also not collected, making it impossible to gauge the prevalence of those with disabilities among the beneficiaries.

Insufficient agency cooperation. In another country, the number of social protection beneficiaries dropped by 3.7% from 2015. This was due to several participating agencies not reporting data, notably those involved with active labor market programs and social assistance.

Source: Compiled by the author from 2022 Social Protection Indicator country reports.

By 2018, the underlying purposes of social protection—support for vulnerable people and commitment to equal opportunities, human rights, and access to services—are enumerated in national policy documents around the region.[9] Most governments provide free or subsidized education, health care, and other basic services, and consider these to be important elements of social protection. Box 2, for example, discusses the services provided by the Government of Kiribati. However, this report follows the ADB definition of social protection, which does not include these

9   I. Ortiz, V. Schmitt, and L. De, eds. 2016. *Social Protection Floors. Vol 1: Universal Schemes.* Geneva: ILO.

universal programs.[10] In fact, another difficulty in analyzing social protection policies and programs in Pacific DMCs is that most DMCs have no clear, formal definition of social protection—either in law or administrative practice. This leads to confusion as to what should be included under social protection programs.

Box 2: Kiribati—Social Protection in a Small Island Developing State

Basic health care in Kiribati is free, while various subsidies in the public (as opposed to private or church) school system are also provided—such as stationery and school fees for primary education. In the past decade, this support has been extended to the secondary school level. The government also subsidizes water and electricity, intra-island shipping, and domestic air travel for all citizens.

Since independence in 1979, major social protection programs have included the National (later Kiribati) Provident Fund and Workmen Compensation Insurance. Until recently, benefits were available only to those employed in the formal sector.

More widely available social protection schemes include the Copra Subsidy Scheme, which assists outer island agriculture producers; Senior Citizens Benefit, a universal old-age benefit; recruitment support for temporary worker schemes in Australia and New Zealand; and school fee assistance for underprivileged children. Only the latter specifically targets the very poor; all other programs disregard income or employment status.

Only six staff members within the Ministry of Women, Youth, Sports and Social Affairs are responsible for the development and promotion of new social protection policies, administration and management of social protection programs, and provision of social services. These are significant responsibilities that hinder their ability to deliver high-quality services and well-informed policy advice.

Source: ADB. 2022. *Kiribati: Social Protection Indicator*. Manila.

In many cases, these new government commitments have been backed up by new policies and laws. In Kiribati, the current development plan and national vision call for more equitable development, and the Employment and Industrial Relations Code was amended in 2016 to include a disability-inclusive policy.[11] Fiji's approach to inclusive development is presented in Box 3. The national development strategy of Solomon Islands outlines the government's plan to develop a social protection policy to address the growing issues of vulnerable population groups, including those with disabilities.[12] In Tonga, a 2016 survey into the situation of people with disabilities and the 2019 Labour Mobility Policy reflect growing recognition of the need to expand assistance and support for vulnerable groups, although this is yet to be demonstrated in budget allocations.[13]

---

[10] ADB. 2012. *The Revised Social Protection Index: Methodology and Handbook*. Manila.

[11] Government of Kiribati. 2016. *Kiribati National Development Plan, 2016–2019*. Tarawa; and Government of Kiribati. 2016. *Kiribati 20-Year Vision, 2016–2036*. Tarawa.

[12] Government of Solomon Islands, Ministry of Development Planning and Aid Coordination. 2011. *National Development Strategy, 2011 to 2020*. Honiara.

[13] Government of Tonga, Ministry of Internal Affairs. 2019. *Tonga Labour Mobility Policy 2019/20–2023/24: A Policy Framework for Enhancing the Development Impact of Labour Mobility in Tonga*. Nuku'alofa; and Government of Tonga, Tonga Statistics Department. 2019. *Disability in Tonga: Analysis of the Situation of People with Disability Based on the 2016 Population and Housing Census*. Nuku'alofa.

Box 3: **Fiji and Inclusive Development**

Since 2014, the Government of Fiji has emphasized the need for more inclusive development and for the removal of inequalities attributed to geographic area, sex, age, disability status, and ethnicity. The government has reinforced this policy direction through the ratification of various international conventions, such as the Convention on the Rights of Persons with Disabilities; legal reforms; reforms to the social assistance system, including introduction of the Poverty Benefit Scheme and Social Pension Scheme; changes to the Fiji National Provident Fund and employment conditions; drafting of national policies, such as the National Policy on Ageing (2017) and National Employment Policy (2018); and changes to various ministries to streamline administration.

This focus has driven the expansion of social protection programs and government spending on them, along with programs that benefit the poor and vulnerable but fall outside of the ADB definition of social protection. These include housing programs, microcredit programs, some educational scholarship programs, and legal aid.

Source: ADB. 2022. *Fiji: Social Protection Indicator*. Manila.

Key Findings from the Social Protection Indicators

The countries referred to in this report are the 14 Pacific DMCs of ADB: the Cook Islands, Fiji, Kiribati, the Marshall Islands, the FSM, Nauru, Niue, Palau, PNG, Samoa, Solomon Islands, Tonga, Tuvalu, and Vanuatu.

These DMCs are all island states in the central Pacific Ocean. They are variously high volcanic islands, raised coral islands, or atolls; and all are highly exposed to various natural hazards, particularly tropical cyclones, as well as risks posed by climate change. As small states and economies, they are also exposed to economic shocks emanating from beyond the region—the most recent brought about by the COVID-19 pandemic.

These DMCs have quite diverse cultures; histories; sizes of their land areas, sea areas, and resources; and levels of social and economic development. The smallest DMCs of the region—Niue and Tuvalu—have populations of 1,600 and 10,600, respectively; the largest, PNG, has a population of almost 9 million.[14]

Economic diversity among the Pacific DMCs is demonstrated in the World Bank classification of country income groups. In 2018, the reference year for this SPI analysis, Palau and Nauru rank as high-income countries; the Cook Islands, Fiji, the Marshall Islands, the FSM, Tonga, and Tuvalu rank as upper middle-income countries; and Kiribati, Samoa, and the larger, resource-rich states of PNG, Solomon Islands, and Vanuatu rank as lower middle-income countries.[15] These rankings,

---

[14]   SPC. 2020. *Pacific Islands Populations 2020*. Noumea.
[15]   World Bank. 2018. *Current Classification of Countries by Income*. Washington, DC.

however, may overstate the economic security in this vulnerable region.[16] Using the Human Development Index (HDI) of the United Nations Development Programme, these countries range from high (i.e., Fiji, the Marshall Islands, Palau, Samoa, and Tonga) to low human development (i.e., PNG and Solomon Islands) (Table 2).[17]

Table 2: Pacific Island Developing Member Countries by Various Development Indicators, 2018

Country	World Bank Country Classification, 2018	UNDP Human Development Index, 2018		ADB Social Protection Indicator, 2018
		HDI	Rank	
Palau	High income	0.798	60	10.4
Nauru	High income		Unlisted	2.9
Niue	High income		Unlisted	7.8
Fiji	Upper middle income	0.741	93	3.3
Cook Islands	Upper middle income		Unlisted	3.3
Tonga	Upper middle income	0.726	98	1.5
Marshall Islands	Upper middle income	0.708	106	10.3
FSM	Upper middle income	0.627	131	5.0
Tuvalu	Upper middle income		Unlisted	10.7
Samoa	Lower middle income	0.713	104	3.4
Kiribati	Lower middle income	0.612	134	11.1
Vanuatu	Lower middle income	0.603	136	3.4
Papua New Guinea	Lower middle income	0.544	151	0.9
Solomon Islands	Lower middle income	0.546	152	3.0

ADB = Asian Development Bank, FSM = Federated States of Micronesia, GNI = gross national income, HDI = Human Development Index, OECD = Organisation for Economic Co-operation and Development, UNDP = United Nations Development Programme.

Notes:

1. The World Bank classification in 2018 is based on national income, as follows: low-income economies with GNI per capita of $1,005 or less in 2016; lower middle-income economies with a GNI per capita between $1,006 and $3,955; upper middle-income economies with a GNI per capita between $3,956 and $12,235; and high-income economies with a GNI per capita of $12,236 or more. The Cook Islands and Nauru are ranked according to the OECD classification.

2. The HDI is a composite index focusing on three basic dimensions of human development: the ability to lead a long and healthy life, measured by life expectancy at birth; ability to acquire knowledge, measured by mean years of schooling and expected years of schooling; and ability to achieve a decent standard of living, as measured by GNI per capita. The HDI ranking is based on 178 participating countries.

Sources: UNDP. 2018. *Human Development Indices and Indicators: 2018 Statistical Update*. New York; and World Bank. 2018. *Current Classification of Countries by Income*. Washington, DC.

---

[16] Niue was not ranked in the World Bank data system. The SPI classified it as high income based on its per capita GDP.

[17] United Nations Development Programme (UNDP). 2018. *Human Development Indices and Indicators: 2018 Statistical Update*. New York; and Sustainable Development Solutions Network. https://www.unsdsn.org/ (accessed 10 October 2021).

Kiribati, the Marshall Islands, Palau, and Tuvalu rank as having among the highest SPIs in the region (Figure 1 and Table 3). Some Pacific DMCs that have low-income and HDI rankings also have low SPIs, with Tonga being a notable exception. As both the HDI and SPI incorporate GDP measurements, a close alignment of these indexes is expected, as the consistent rankings of the HDI and GDP demonstrate. More influential than the size of GDP on the types and distribution of social protection programs in each DMC is its own history of social policies, policy decisions, or remaining eligibility for or access to social protection programs in other countries to which they were once tied.

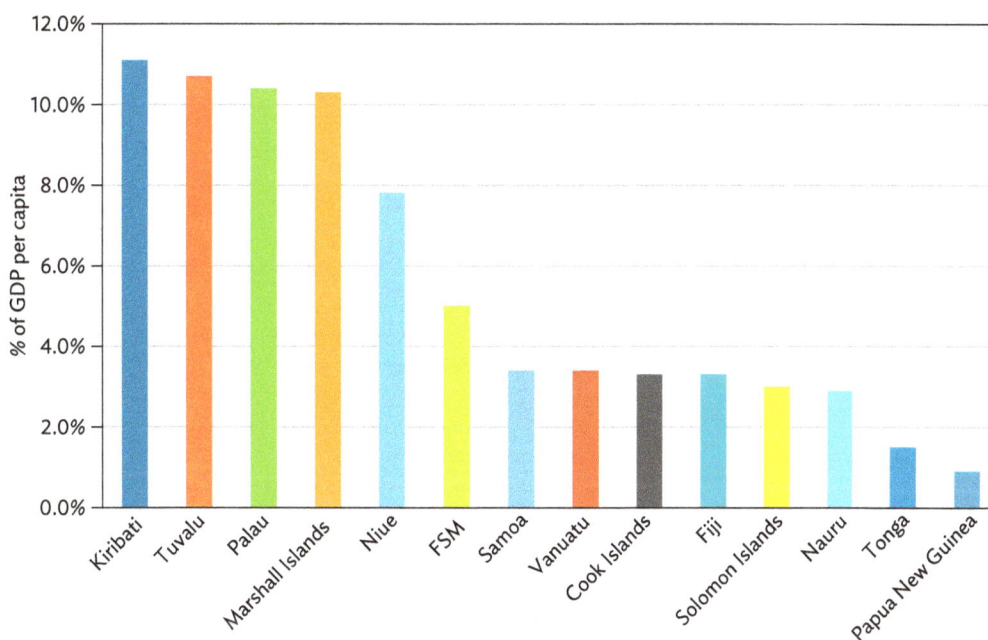

Figure 1: **Countries Ranked by Social Protection Indicator, 2018**

FSM = Federated States of Micronesia, GDP = gross domestic product.
Source: ADB estimates, 2018, based on consultants' reports.

The DMC with the highest SPI is Kiribati. This reflects considerable investment in social assistance and active labor market programs over the past decade, particularly support to informal sector producers.

Pacific DMCs have strong traditions of family and communities looking after one another in difficult times. Thus, some view raising social protection in national policy discussions, as well as poverty and vulnerability issues, as a dismissal of local culture and traditions. It has been argued that spending on social protection could erode cultural values, compete with spending on "real" development such as infrastructure and services, or perversely reward people who put the least effort into their own welfare. Yet in a fast-changing world, Pacific island communities have come under new, intense pressures, as have many small and vulnerable societies around the world.

Table 3: Social Protection Indicator by Category, 2018
(% of GDP per capita)

	Overall	Social Insurance	Social Assistance	Labor Market Programs
Cook Islands	3.3	0.5	2.8	...
Fiji	3.3	2.2	1.1	0.0
Kiribati	11.1	3.7	0.9	6.5
Marshall Islands	10.3	8.3	0.9	1.1
FSM	5.0	4.2	0.8	...
Nauru	2.9	0.1	2.8	...
Niue	7.8	1.1	6.7	...
Palau	10.4	9.2	1.1	0.1
Papua New Guinea	0.9	0.9	...	0.0
Samoa	3.4	2.4	0.9	0.1
Solomon Islands	3.0	2.9	0.0	0.1
Tonga	1.5	1.0	0.4	0.1
Tuvalu	10.7	3.7	7.0	...
Vanuatu	3.4	0.9	2.5	0.0
Unweighted Pacific Average	**5.5**	**2.9**	**2.0**	**0.6**

... = no data, 0.0 = less than 0.1%, FSM = Federated States of Micronesia, GDP = gross domestic product.

Source: ADB estimates, 2018, based on consultants' country reports.

For instance, the Fiji government has made considerable effort over the past decade to expand the availability of social protection for its citizens and better provide for low-income and other disadvantaged people.

HIESs and poverty analyses throughout the Pacific region have found that many households are indeed vulnerable to poverty—well beyond just the chronically poor—and that a single adverse event or shift in circumstances can trap these households into long-term poverty.[18]

---

[18]   For example, see AusAID. 2012. Social Cohesion and Social Protection in Pacific Island Countries. *AusAID Pacific Social Protection Series: Poverty, Vulnerability and Social Protection in the Pacific.* Canberra; A. Moustafa. 2015. *Nauru Hardship and Poverty Report: Analysis of the 2012/13 Household Income and Expenditure Survey.* Suva: UNDP Pacific Centre; Development Pathways and Government of the Cook Islands. 2020. The State of Poverty and Vulnerability in the Cook Islands: Challenges and Recommendations. Draft; K. Fisk and J. Crawford. 2017. *Exploring Multidimensional Poverty in Fiji: Findings from a Study Using the Individual Deprivation Measure.* Suva: International Women's Development Agency and Fiji Bureau of Statistics; and World Bank. 2020. *Equity and Poverty Brief: Kiribati.* Washington, DC.

II. Expenditure on Social Protection in the Pacific Region

Overall Social Protection Expenditure as Share of Gross Domestic Product

Social protection expenditure grew substantially in several Pacific DMCs from 2009 to 2018, particularly the Cook Islands, Fiji, and Solomon Islands (Table 4). SPI values rose in most DMCs but less than expenditures; indeed, fast GDP growth biases SPI growth downward. The SPI is also measured in relation to the number of beneficiaries—a number that can be raised or lowered not just by program design but also by demographic trends, such as changes to the population age structure and employment and migration rates.

Table 4: Growth in per Capita Gross Domestic Product, 2009–2018

Country	GDP per Capita ($)				Growth (%)
	2009	2012	2015	2018	2012–2018
Solomon Islands	1,052	1,504	1,748	2,203	46.5
Cook Islands	...	17,126	16,664	23,550	37.5
Fiji	3,758	4,534	5,052	6,232	37.4
Papua New Guinea	490	2,151	1,990	2,676	24.4
Palau	10,131	13,341	16,273	16,304	22.2
FSM	...	3,192	3,079	3,855	20.8
Marshall Islands	2,838	3,467	3,326	4,056	17.0
Samoa	2,907	3,635	4,001	4,150	14.2
Tonga	...	4,494	3,795	4,874	8.5
Vanuatu	2,471	3,027	2,722	3,207	5.9
Kiribati	...	1,772	1,472	1,767	(0.3)
Nauru	5,313	11,946	8,150	10,910	(8.7)
Niue	...	...	...	18,462	
Tuvalu	...	...	...	4,714	

... = no data, ( ) = negative, FSM = Federated States of Micronesia, GDP = gross domestic product.

Source: ADB estimates based on 2022 Social Protection Indicator country reports.

In 2018, social protection expenditure in the 14 Pacific DMCs average 6.0% of their GDPs. Relative to their GDPs, the DMCs with the highest expenditure on social protection are Palau (14.1%), Kiribati (12.0%), the Marshall Islands (11.6%), and Tuvalu (11.4%)—which all have high rates even by global standards. Some DMCs with social protection spending close to the average—Niue (8.4%), Fiji (4.3%), and the Cook Islands (4.0%)—demonstrate that with these levels of expenditure, sizable social protection can be provided. Those that spend the smallest share of their GDPs on social protection are Solomon Islands (2.2%), Tonga (1.7%), and PNG (1.0%). Expenditure for each intended beneficiary as a share of GDP per capita—in other words, the SPI—is highest in Kiribati (11.1%), Tuvalu (10.7%), and Palau (10.4%), and lowest in Nauru (2.9%), Tonga (1.5%), and PNG (0.9%) (Figure 2).

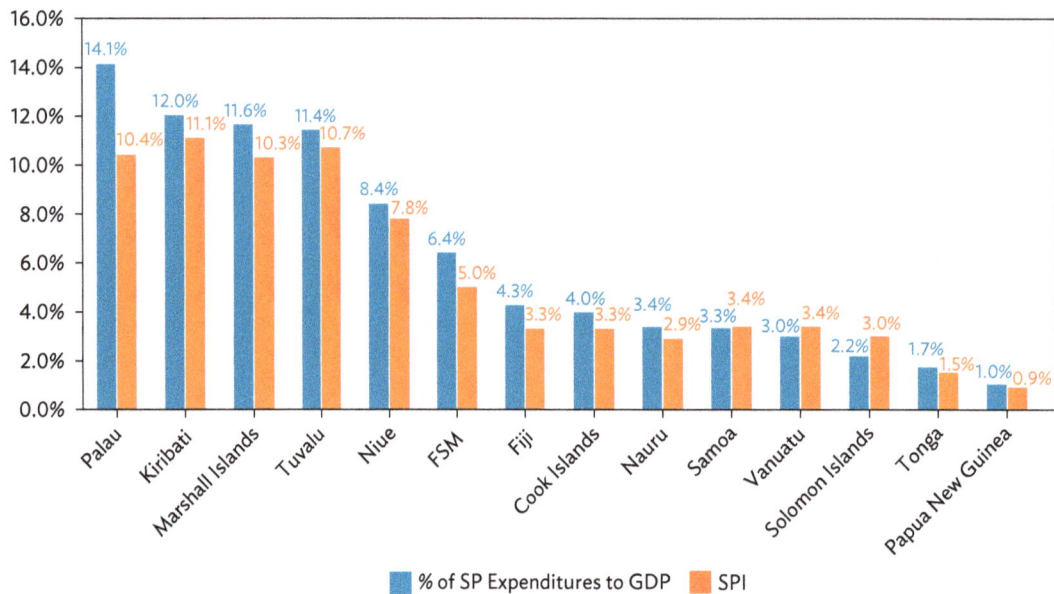

Figure 2: Share of Gross Domestic Product Spent on Social Protection, 2018

FSM = Federated States of Micronesia, GDP = gross domestic product, SP = social protection, SPI = Social Protection Indicator.

Source: ADB estimates based on consultants' country reports.

In their income group classifications, the upper middle-income countries (i.e., Fiji, the Marshall Islands, the FSM, Tonga, and Tuvalu) have an average SPI of 6.2% of GDP per capita, higher than the regional average of 5.5% and that of the high-income countries of the region (i.e., the Cook Islands, Nauru, and Palau) at 6.1%. The lower middle-income countries (i.e., Kiribati, PNG, Samoa, Solomon Islands, and Vanuatu) have an average SPI of 4.3% (Figure 3).

When the DMCs are grouped according to their incomes, the pattern of expenditure by category changes, mostly in respect to the dominance of social insurance and the size of active LMPs. High-income and upper middle-income countries generally spend more on social insurance and social assistance than lower middle-income countries, but there are many exceptions. On average, lower middle-income countries spend the

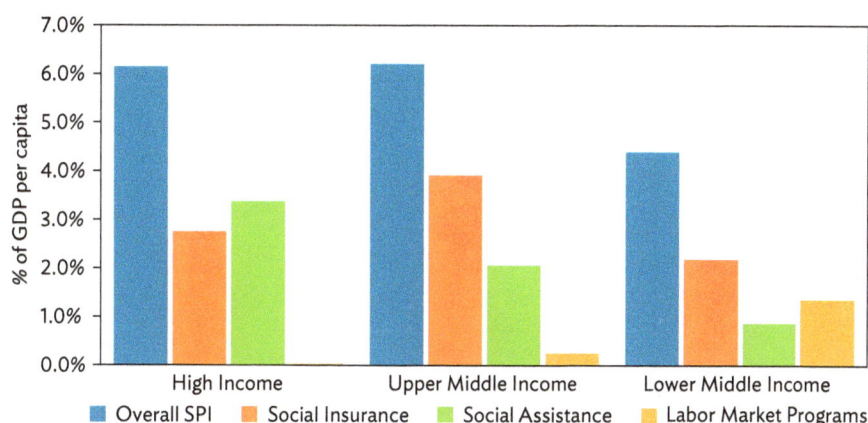

Figure 3: Social Protection Indicator by Income Status, 2018

GDP = gross domestic product, SPI = Social Protection Indicator.

Note: The countries are ranked by World Bank country income classification except for Nauru, which is ranked according to the Organisation for Economic Co-operation and Development classification.

Source: ADB estimates based on consultants' country reports.

most on active LMPs, an average lifted by Kiribati and its merchant seafarer training, job placement programs, and cash for work from the copra price subsidy program.[19]

However, no clear patterns are evident when the SPI situation is analyzed in this manner—there is no tight association between a country's GDP and its spending on social protection. As Table 5 shows, at the same income level, some countries invest much more in social protection than others. It is sometimes assumed that only wealthy countries can afford well-developed social protection systems, but this is not true. Affordability may be more of a national expectation of an acceptable standard of living, or political will to redress unequal development.

In fact, the DMC with the highest SPI is Kiribati. Kiribati has invested a good share of the returns from recent economic growth into LMP, especially for outer island communities through its Copra Subsidy Scheme.[20] The DMC with the second-highest SPI, Palau, is one of the wealthiest DMCs of the region, with a per capita income of $16,265 in 2018 (Table 4). Solomon Islands is an anomaly, as its SPI of 3.0% of GDP per capita is almost totally due to its social insurance as its national provident fund dwarfs its other social protection programs but has far fewer beneficiaries, giving them high per capita benefits.[21]

---

[19] The appendix contains tables that enable comparison by country.

[20] Nominally a lower middle-income country, Kiribati also has a substantial sovereign wealth fund, the Revenue Equalization Reserve Fund, established in the 1950s to hold surplus royalties from phosphate mining, which provides regular contributions to the annual budget. The fund value was A$1.17 billion at the end of September 2020. ADB. 2022. *Kiribati: Social Protection Indicator*. Manila.

[21] In 2018, benefits from social insurance in Solomon Islands averaged SI$53.33, compared with SI$0.04 from social assistance and SI$7.23 from active LMP programs (Table 5).

Table 5: Social Protection Indicator by Social Protection and Income Category, 2018
(% of GDP per capita)

	Overall SPI	Social Insurance	Social Assistance	Labor Market programs
High Income				
Cook Islands	3.3	0.5	2.8	...
Nauru	2.9	0.1	2.8	...
Niue	7.8	1.1	6.7	...
Palau	10.4	9.2	1.1	0.1
Unweighted Average	**6.1**	**2.7**	**3.4**	**0.0**
Upper Middle Income				
Fiji	3.3	2.2	1.1	0.0
Marshall Islands	10.3	8.3	0.9	1.1
FSM	5.0	4.2	0.8	...
Tonga	1.5	1.0	0.4	0.1
Tuvalu	10.7	3.7	7.0	...
Unweighted Average	**6.2**	**3.9**	**2.0**	**0.2**
Lower Middle Income				
Kiribati	11.1	3.7	0.9	6.5
Papua New Guinea	0.9	0.9	...	0.0
Samoa	3.4	2.4	0.9	0.1
Solomon Islands	3.0	2.9	0.0	0.1
Vanuatu	3.4	0.9	2.5	0.0
Unweighted Average	**4.4**	**2.2**	**0.9**	**1.3**
Unweighted Pacific Average	**5.5**	**2.9**	**2.0**	**0.6**

... = no data, 0.0 = value is less than 0.1, FSM = Federated States of Micronesia, GDP = gross domestic product, SPI = Social Protection Indicator.

Note: Countries are ranked according to World Bank classifications, except for the Cook Islands, which is classified by Organisation for Economic Co-operation and Development criteria.

Source: ADB estimates based on consultants' country reports.

Furthermore, government and other national expenditures do not tell the whole story about the availability of social protection benefits. Today, these Pacific DMCs are independent states, but some maintain close connections with countries to which they were once tied (i.e., the Cook Islands and Niue to New Zealand, and the FSM, the Marshall Islands, and Palau to the United States [US]). Through their continuing associations, some benefits remain available to these Pacific DMCs. The Marshall Islands, the FSM, and Palau have Compacts of Free Association with the US, providing them with significant budget and development aid that includes eligibility for some US-based social assistance programs, as well as open entry to the US for citizens. Niue and the Cook Islands have similar relationships with New Zealand, as their residents hold New Zealand citizenship and have open entry to both New Zealand and Australia and eligibility for New Zealand social protection program benefits.

In regard to access to US-based social assistance programs, most social assistance programs in the Marshall Islands, the FSM, and Palau are funded by US federal grants or are legacies of such grants, which were phased out after implementation of the compacts and subsequently absorbed into national government budgets.[22] For example, the FSM has no government-funded social assistance programs of its own, but under the US Individuals with Disabilities Education Act, the FSM Department of Education receives funding from the US Department of Education to supplement special education and related services for children ages 0 to 21 years with disabilities.[23]

Moreover, since its independence in 1965, the Cook Islands has had comprehensive social assistance programs, such as the Child Benefit and Old Age Pension, that were closely modeled on those of the New Zealand welfare system. In addition, as New Zealand citizens, the Cook Islanders have the right to live and work in both New Zealand and Australia; thus, there are high levels of outmigration to these countries for employment, study, and other opportunities. As New Zealand superannuation and social assistance programs have loosened their eligibility requirements, many Cook Islanders end up returning to the Cook Islands but are able to retain their New Zealand social assistance benefit payments.[24]

Another example is the government pension programs in the Marshall Islands, the FSM, and Palau, established in the late 1960s by the Government of the Trust Territory of the Pacific Islands and patterned after the US Social Security program.[25] In Fiji, a small, means-tested social assistance program continued with little structural change from before its independence from the United Kingdom in 1970 until a government and World Bank review in 2011. Since then, the Ministry of Women, Children and Poverty Alleviation has been restructured, a new national poverty eradication program was introduced, and a broader array of social assistance and poverty alleviation benefits are provided—particularly for people with disabilities.[26]

Beyond this, all Pacific DMCs have high levels of international donor assistance, much of which is directed to reinforcing basic services and social well-being—helping improve program effectiveness but rarely contributing directly to social protection payments. Many social services are also provided by civil society organizations (CSOs), nongovernment organizations (NGOs), and churches, supported to some extent by governments and international or local donors. Box 4, for example, discusses international support in Papua New Guinea. More informally, family networks provide other sources of support; remittances often constitute a significant amount of household income. In Tonga, for example, remittances and gifts provide 20% of household income—second only to employment income at 65%—and constitute 30% of GDP.[27]

DMCs where the largest share of their social protection expenditure derives from social insurance are PNG (99.0%), Solomon Islands (98.2%), Palau (87.5%), and the FSM (84.9%). DMCs with the smallest share of their social protection expenditure going to social insurance are Nauru (4.1%), the Cook Islands (13.7%), and Niue (14.3%) (Figure 4).

---

[22] ADB. 2022. *Palau: Social Protection Indicator*. Manila.
[23] ADB. 2022. *Federated States of Micronesia: Social Protection Indicator*. Manila.
[24] ADB. 2022. *Cook Islands: Social Protection Indicator*. Manila.
[25] ADB. 2022. *Palau: Social Protection Indicator*. Manila.
[26] World Bank. 2011. *Assessment of the Social Protection System in Fiji and Recommendations for Policy Changes.* Washington, DC; and ADB. 2022. *Fiji: Social Protection Indicator*. Manila.
[27] ADB. 2022. *Tonga: Social Protection Indicator*. Manila.

Box 4: Papua New Guinea and International Support

Primero, an innovative information management program, was launched in 2018 by the Government of Papua New Guinea to help protect vulnerable women and children, particularly survivors of domestic violence. Primero assists social welfare staff in managing protection- and violence-related cases and improving data collection and analysis. It thereby strengthens the implementation of the Lukautim Pikinini Act 2015, which focuses on child protection and prevention of gender-based violence.

Primero has been supported from its outset by the United Nations Children's Fund (UNICEF), other United Nations agencies, and Australia's Department of Foreign Affairs and Trade. It is also supported by the European Union through the Spotlight Initiative, a partnership between the European Union and United Nations, which aims to eliminate all forms of violence against women and girls.

Source: ADB. 2022. *Papua New Guinea: Social Protection Indicator*. Manila.

Figure 4: Social Protection Expenditure for Social Insurance
(% of total SP expenditure)

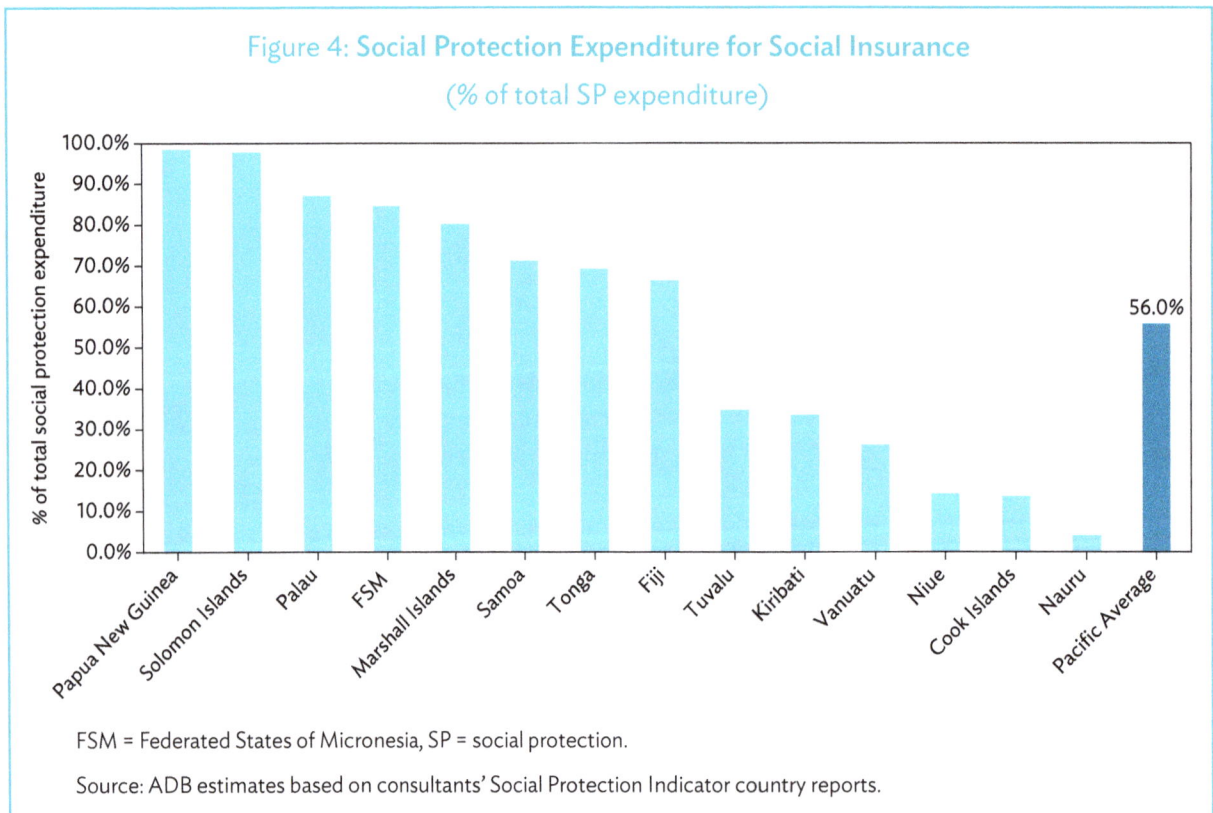

FSM = Federated States of Micronesia, SP = social protection.

Source: ADB estimates based on consultants' Social Protection Indicator country reports.

Figure 5 shows that the DMCs that allocate the largest part of their social protection expenditures to social assistance are Nauru (95.9%), Niue (85.7%), the Cook Islands (86.3%), and Vanuatu (72.8%). Apart from PNG, which has virtually no social assistance, DMCs that allocate the smallest shares are Solomon Islands (0.1%), Tonga (0.4%), Kiribati (7.9%), the Marshall Islands (8.7%), and Palau (10.5%). The Marshall Islands, the FSM, and Palau, however, do have access to some US social assistance programs.

Figure 5: Social Protection Expenditure for Social Assistance

(% of total SP expenditure)

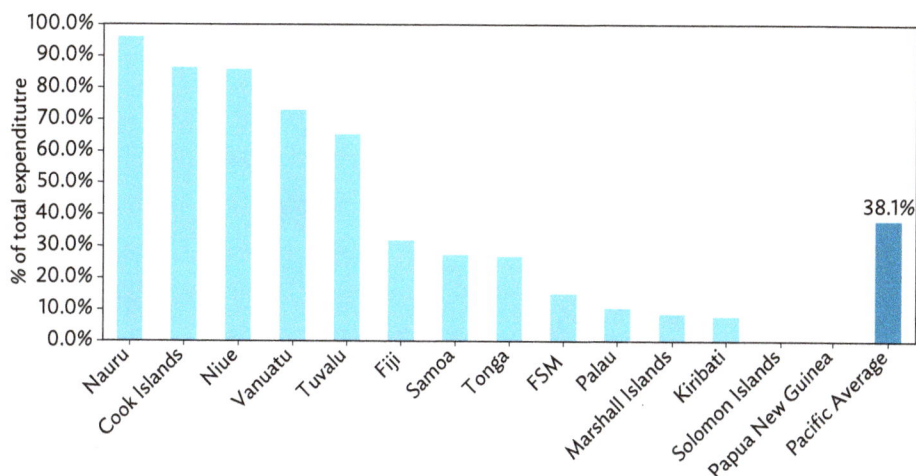

FSM = Federated States of Micronesia, SP = social protection.

Source: ADB estimates based on consultants' country reports.

DMCs with the largest shares of expenditure on active LMPs are Kiribati (58.4%), the Marshall Islands (10.8%), and Tonga (3.7%). Several DMCs spent very little on active LMPs, such as PNG and Vanuatu. No LMPs are reported in the Cook Islands, the FSM, Nauru, Niue, and Tuvalu (Figure 6).

Figure 6: Social Protection Expenditure on Labor Market Programs, 2018

(% of total SP expenditure)

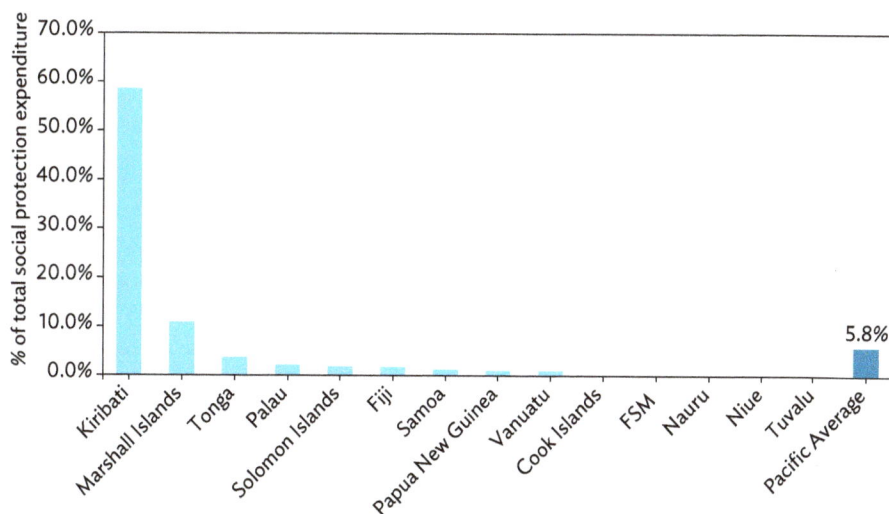

FSM = Federated States of Micronesia, SP = social protection.

Source: ADB estimates based on consultants' country reports.

Social Protection Indicator by Category

1. Social Insurance

Of the three categories of social protection, social insurance has the largest SPI, a pattern that has long held in the Pacific region. In 2018, the social insurance SPI accounted for a regional average of 2.9% of per capita GDP, higher than that spent on social assistance (an average of 2.0%) and a little more than three times that spent on active LMPs (an average of 0.6%) (Figure 7).

Figure 7: Social Protection Indicator by Category, 2018

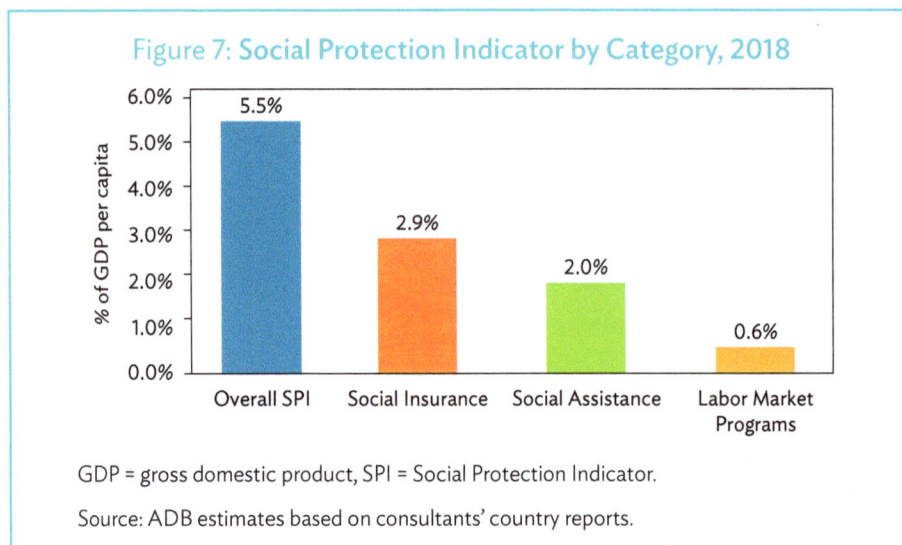

GDP = gross domestic product, SPI = Social Protection Indicator.

Source: ADB estimates based on consultants' country reports.

Pensions. Social insurance programs are contributory schemes intended to help people manage common risks such as illness, old age, and unemployment. They mostly involve pensions or provident funds for people ages 60 and older. Most recipients are those who are or have been in formal employment, with some schemes tailored to the public sector but most to both public and private sector employees. Retirees can receive their provident fund retirement benefits either as a lump-sum payment or, in some countries, a monthly pension. These schemes usually also provide loans for certain purposes and one-off benefits, such as death benefits paid to families of deceased members to assist with funeral expenses. Other social insurance programs include health insurance, and other insurance schemes such as provident funds, unemployment insurance, and worker compensation schemes. In contributory schemes, higher-earning people receive more benefits, making these programs neither pro-poor nor "pro" other forms of social equitability, particularly not by sex or disability status.

In some Pacific DMCs, contributory pensions are complemented with universal, non-contributory old-age pensions (i.e., a form of social assistance). Together, these retirement schemes are coming under pressure in several DMCs due to the rapid aging of the population and slower-than-forecast growth of paid employment, a problem sometimes compounded by poor fund management. The Fiji National Provident Fund underwent a major restructuring of benefits in 2013 to protect its sustainability. In the FSM, where growth in formal employment has lagged, the FSM Social Security Administration faces a growing gap between contributions received and the cost of benefit payments and administrative expenses.[28] Similarly, in Palau, the Civil Service Pension Trust Fund was under financial strain in 2019, its long-standing problem of underfunded contributions exacerbated by high debt levels and global economic trends, with calls for urgent reforms to improve its sustainability.[29]

In Nauru, the Superannuation Fund stopped paying out pensions in 2005. All payments are now drawn from the government budget at a baseline figure of A$140 per fortnight, as respective governments ponder how this public fund may be cleared. Meanwhile, the Ex-Members of Parliament Pension, which is a noncontributory allowance for ex-members of parliament, also pays its benefits through the national budget, distributing an average payment of A$9,738 in 2018 to each of the 12 eligible beneficiaries, equivalent to 92% of Nauru's GDP per capita.[30]

In Fiji, opportunities for social insurance have been broadened through government-financed programs, with increased allowances for worker compensation as provided in occupational health and safety legislation introduced in 2014 as well as the expanded Fiji Ex-Servicemen's After Care Fund to address health repercussions from active military service. This fund provides allowances for retired people who have served overseas and to their widows and other survivors, including special grants for medical assistance and loans for their children's education. Formed in 1944 and intended for Republic of Fiji Military Forces personnel who served in World War II, the fund was progressively widened to veterans of other foreign campaigns. In 2018, membership was extended to include all police and correctional officers. This expansion of membership, as well as allocations, have increased its significance in social insurance in Fiji.[31] Similarly, in PNG, the Defence Force Retirement Benefit Fund provides retirement benefits to Defence Force personnel and their dependents upon discharge or death.[32] Following a review of the fund by the Bank of Papua New Guinea in 2021, legislation allowed the fund to open membership beyond the PNG Defence Force to include other employers, allowing the fund to grow.[33]

---

[28] ADB. 2022. *Federated States of Micronesia: Social Protection Indicator.* Manila.
[29] A recent audit showed a pension liability nearly 10 times the size of fund assets, threatening full depletion of the fund by FY2022. R. Rabanal. 2019. Palau: Reforming the Civil Service Pension Plan. In ADB. *Pacific Economic Monitor.* July. Manila.
[30] ADB. 2012. *Nauru: Updating and Improving the Social Protection Index.* Consultant's report. Manila.
[31] D. Baleniabuli. 2019. Ageing: An Analysis of Government Policies for Older Persons in Fiji (Pre- and Post-Independence). Unpublished; and Government of Fiji, Ministry of Defence and National Security. 2015. Government to Disburse Funds to Veterans of Christmas Island Operations "Grapple." Press release. 29 January. Suva.
[32] ADB. 2022. *Papua New Guinea: Social Protection Indicator.* Manila.
[33] C. Patjole. 2021. CTSL to Open DFRBF Membership. *LOOP.* 18 April. https://www.facebook.com/looppng/.

The main difficulties in providing social insurance to informal sector workers and other people with low or irregular incomes are (i) making these payments affordable; and (ii) addressing the high administrative costs of managing small, irregular payments. Through its Micro-Insurance Policy, the Government of Fiji has bypassed these problems by operating the scheme through a private company and paying all premiums for eligible participants (Box 5). In addition, in 2018, the Vanuatu National Provident Fund established the Informal Sector Unit to cater to voluntary contributions from self-employed and informal sector workers (Box 6).[34]

Box 5: Social Insurance for the Low-Income Population in Fiji

Introduced in 2017, Fiji's microinsurance is a new insurance scheme for low-income people, providing them—for the first time—with some insurance coverage. The government pays the premiums, offering a proxy cash benefit to participating households. Operated by a private company, FijiCare, it provides insurance for all social assistance recipients, as well as for civil servants, including funeral expenses and injury and personal accident insurance, covering a total of F$10,000 per insured person at a cost of F$52 per year or F$1 per week.

The program helps address the low insurance penetration rate in Fiji of only 12%. Most low-income households lack any form of protection against adverse events, as they cannot afford standard premiums, and the income generated from this pool would be very low.

Source: ADB. 2022. *Fiji: Social Protection Indicator*. Manila.

Box 6: Vanuatu National Provident Fund and the Informal Sector

Access to formal financial services is restricted in Vanuatu, as over 80% of its working population is employed in the informal sector. In 2018, the Vanuatu National Provident Fund (VNPF) conducted a feasibility study of the demand, interest, and willingness of informal sector Ni-Vanuatu to contribute to superannuation or pension schemes. A positive response led to the VNPF establishing its Informal Sector Unit and a mobile service that now serves informal sector workers in urban and rural areas. In 2020, over 200 new self-employed or informal sector workers registered as members of the VNPF, including market vendors, house girls, gardeners, handicraft workers, farmers, and fishers—people who otherwise had little, if any, access to retirement savings or other benefits such as loans or death benefits. The VNPF plans to extend these services to include medical insurance and house insurance to help cover cyclone-related damages.

Sources: K. Kalsakau and A. Roberts. 2020. Over 200 Informal Workers Registered with VNPF. *Vanuatu Daily Post*. 24 November. https://www.dailypost.vu/news/over-200-informal-workers-registered-with-vnpf/article_0390c000-2ddc-11eb-a0f7-53708eb9f1ed.html; and UNDP Pacific Office. 2018. VNPF to Study Micro-Pensions for Vanuatu's Informal Sector. Press release. 11 October. https://www.undp.org/pacific/press-releases/vnpf-study-micro-pensions-vanuatu%E2%80%99s-informal-sector.

---

[34]   ILO. 2021. Innovation to Increase Access to Social Security in Vanuatu. ILO in the Pacific. https://www.ilo.org/suva/public-information/WCMS_818273/lang--en/index.htm.

Health insurance. The lack of universal health insurance in most Pacific DMCs has been addressed through the provision of free or low-cost public health services.[35] In Samoa, for example, the national health assistance program accounts for a significant part of social assistance.[36] A 2016 study in Fiji found that the distribution of health-care benefits there slightly favored the poor. About 61% of public spending for nursing stations and 26% of spending for public hospital inpatient care went toward services provided to the poorest 20% of the population. The poor thereby received a higher share of benefits from government health spending and bore a lower share of the financing burden than did wealthier groups.[37] These services, however, provide for health care, not the full consequences of ill health, such as unemployment or death of a breadwinner.

2.   Social Assistance

Social assistance accounts for smaller SPIs, with a regional average of only 2.0% of GDP per capita, most of which is focused on social assistance for specific groups of disadvantaged people (Figure 7).

Social assistance programs provide noncontributory cash or in-kind transfers to defined groups of people, such as the poor, older persons, or people with disabilities. Periodic increases in eligibility criteria and payments account for some of the amplified expenditure on social assistance programs, but the region has also witnessed investment in a wider range of services. Most programs are relatively small, provide low benefits per beneficiary, and are tightly targeted—although this is slowly changing. Universal programs are growing, for which there are important advantages, including much lower administrative costs, less red tape for applicants, less difficulty in identifying recipients, and clearer recognition that all citizens have equal rights to public services and to full social inclusion.

In DMCs where only small social assistance programs exist, traditional family support systems are assumed to adequately protect the vulnerable. Yet there is good evidence—even in the most traditional societies—that this often is not so. In Tonga, for example, where the strength of family and community support is reflected in high remittances from Tongans living abroad, a 2018 study found that one in three children and one in four adults live in poverty.[38]

Fiji's two main social assistance programs—the Poverty Benefit Scheme (PBS) and Social Pension Scheme (SPS)—represent the highest social protection expenditure in the country. The PBS is available to impoverished households, providing them with monthly cash payments and food vouchers, for which eligibility is limited to a

---

[35] Regarding health-care expenditure in the Pacific region, 82% was paid for by governments, a further 8% came from private contributions or out-of-pocket payments, and the rest was derived from foreign aid. J. Pryke, A. Dayant, and T. Izumi. 2021. Health Spending and Foreign Aid in the Pacific. *The Interpreter.* 8 October. https://www.lowyinstitute.org/the-interpreter/health-spending-and-foreign-aid-pacific.

[36] ADB. 2022. *Samoa: Social Protection Indicator.* Manila.

[37] A. Asante et al. 2016. Financing for Universal Health Coverage in Small Island States: Evidence from the Fiji Islands. *BMJ Global Health.* 2 (2).

[38] ADB. 2022. *Tonga: Social Protection Indicator.* Manila.

maximum of 3 years. For the SPS, people over age 65 years who have no source of income or superannuation are eligible, providing a monthly payment of F$100 in 2018. Through Fiji's Care and Protection Allowance, cash grants and food vouchers are provided to children in single-parent households with low incomes, children with older persons as caregivers, children with disabilities, and children in residential care homes. Other programs such as the disability allowance, rural pregnant mothers food voucher program, and bus fare program are also available to impoverished households. The Housing Authority of Fiji, the Public Rental Board, and the Housing Assistance and Relief Trust, provide affordable housing to low-income households.[39]

PNG does not have any social assistance programs, but under the National Refugee Policy, special assistance is provided to refugees and people who have been displaced by local conflicts. They are assisted in finding employment and in supporting themselves through a range of benefits, including language and cultural orientation programs, case management support, and provision of citizenship. As well as these direct benefits, the government operates programs to address underlying drivers of conflicts, conduct training activities, and formulate community peace plans, working principally with women and youth in rural and remote communities where people are marginalized by displacement, there is low socioeconomic development, and tribal conflicts and human rights abuses are common.

Many DMCs have developed some sort of special assistance for children and adults with disabilities to provide them with minimum income and opportunities to participate in the community. These programs include cash transfer programs, health insurance, special medical assistance, mobility and housing assistance, and disability pensions. Almost all DMCs provide some form of special education services for children with disabilities, although these are often restricted to urban areas. Many also provide grants to persons with disabilities who meet the requirements of some form of national registration.

Services for people with disabilities have long been operated by CSOs and NGOs, with governments providing some funds but also using international donor assistance as well as local donor support. In Samoa, for example, the Inclusive Special Needs Programme is implemented through the Ministry of Education, Sports and Culture, which channels funds to organizations such as Fia Malamalama School, Loto Taumafai Society for People with Disabilities, Nuanua O Le Alofa, Samoa Blind Persons Association, Samoa Victim Support Group School of Hope, and Senese Inclusive Education.[40] In Tonga, no direct child benefits are provided, except for in-kind support for infants with disabilities until they reach age 5 years.[41] Assistance programs for people with disabilities are discussed in depth in Chapter IV.

Apart from benefits provided to the very poor, people with disabilities, or other specific groups, most child assistance programs in most DMCs are universal. The Cook Islands (see Box 7 on the Cook Islands) and Niue provide monthly cash allowances

---

[39]   ADB. 2022. *Fiji: Social Protection Indicator*. Manila.
[40]   ADB. 2022. *Samoa: Social Protection Indicator*. Manila.
[41]   ADB. 2022. *Tonga: Social Protection Indicator*. Manila.

to all children who are resident citizens. Many programs of child social assistance help facilitate school attendance. Nauru has a school-feeding program, while the Marshall Islands, the FSM, and Palau provide head-start and school-feeding programs to improve child nutrition and education outcomes, increase enrollment rates, and reduce absenteeism. These DMCs—plus the Cook Islands, Fiji, and Niue—also provide students with free bus transport to and from school. In 2017–2018, the Government of Nauru introduced an education assistance scheme that provides A$5 for each day a student attends school, the sum of which is paid out when the student graduates from secondary school, the aim being to raise school completion rates.[42] In PNG, some provincial governments also pay all school fees.[43] In 2015, Vanuatu introduced a family protection program and infant-feeding program, neither of them universal but intended to assist broadly defined groups, such as rural children or those vulnerable due to family violence or hardship.

Box 7: The Cook Islands Child Benefit

In the Cook Islands, the Child Benefit is a universal payment for which all children, ages 0 to 14 years, who are resident citizens in the country, are eligible. The benefit, of NZ$100 in 2018, is paid monthly to a child's parent or guardian.

As most paid work in the Cook Island is in Rarotonga, parents working there often send children to the outer islands to be looked after by their grandparents, who then receive the benefit on behalf of the child. The transfer of children and payments is of great value to the outer island communities, helping maintain their social and economic life, support local schools and other services, and ensure that the Cook Islands culture and values are conveyed to a new generation.

Sources: ADB. 2022. *Cook Islands: Social Protection Indicator*. Manila; and Government of the Cook Islands, Ministry of Internal Affairs. 2010. *Review of the Social Welfare System*. Avarua.

Most social assistance to adults is targeted to especially disadvantaged people—but in many DMCs, the scope of these beneficiaries is widening. Since 2015, for example, the Government of Fiji has provided the Food Voucher Programme to pregnant women in rural areas to help improve their nutrition and reduce later-stage pregnancy complications. From 2018, the Parenthood Assistance Payment of F$1,000 has helped low-income families with the costs of raising a newborn. Since 2006, the Government of Nauru has also provided a newborn allowance to new mothers as well as a birth allowance, the latter providing a one-off payment of A$100 intended to help new mothers purchase necessities for their child. To claim this, the mother must submit documentation issued by the hospital to complete the birth registration process, thereby also upgrading the quality of birth registration records.

Despite the critical role of paid employment in averting hardship and poverty, high levels of both hidden and open unemployment throughout the region, and an estimated

---

[42]   Students with disabilities who attend the Able/Disable Centre are exempted from this scheme on the grounds that they do not graduate. ADB. 2022. *Nauru: Social Protection Indicator*. Manila.

[43]   ADB. 2022. *Papua New Guinea: Social Protection Indicator*. Manila.

25% of workers engaged in vulnerable employment,[44] unemployment benefits are rare in Pacific DMCs. Several governments have introduced unemployment benefits on a temporary basis during the COVID-19 pandemic, however. In Kiribati, for example, an unemployment benefit introduced in 2020 amounted to a monthly payment of A\$50 for unemployed people ages 18 to 59 years.[45]

Most DMCs provide some subsidized or free services to all older citizens. In Fiji, all older people are entitled to a bus fare subsidy. The Cook Islands, Kiribati, Nauru, Niue, Samoa, and Tonga provide universal monthly payments to older persons, which are sometimes supplemented with other benefits (e.g., in Tonga, special one-off payments were made after Cyclone Gita in 2018, in celebration of King Tupou VI's 60th birthday in 2019, and as assistance during the COVID-19 pandemic in 2020). The elderly allowance in Nauru supports older people aged 60 and above, offering a higher rate to those aged 70 or older (Box 8). In Samoa, a monthly ST135 pension comes from the Senior Citizens Benefit Scheme, and all resident citizens over age 65 years are eligible for the elderly boat fare, which covers interisland travel, as well as a medical subsidy, which provides free care in public health facilities and free medicines. The government of Palau supports the home care needs of older people without income (Box 9).

Box 8: The Elderly Allowance in Nauru

In Nauru, the Elderly Allowance was introduced in 2005 for people ages 60 years and above as an effort to alleviate economic pressures on older persons. The fortnightly allowance was initially A\$50 and was raised to A\$150 in 2013. In 2015, two new rates were introduced: A\$200 per fortnight for people ages 60 to 69 years, and A\$250 per fortnight for people ages 70 or older. People with other sources of income, including other social assistance benefits, are not eligible for the allowance. In 2018, there were 454 beneficiaries, up from 302 in 2015, a 50% increase.

Source: ADB. 2022. *Nauru: Social Protection Indicator*. Manila.

In the Cook Islands, the Old Age Pension increased from NZ\$600 to NZ\$660 per month in 2016. In addition, as mentioned previously, New Zealand superannuation rules were amended in 2018, waiving the requirement for recipients to reside in New Zealand for 10 years after age 60 years. Thus, around 200 people switched from the Cook Islands Old Age Pension to the New Zealand pension after returning to the Cook Islands, for which payments are notably larger.[46]

3.   Labor Market Programs

An even smaller share of social protection expenditure is directed to active LMPs in the Pacific DMCs. The SPI for active LMPs in 2018 is only 0.6% of GDP per capita in the Pacific, providing less than one-tenth of the overall SPI for the Pacific. There are, again, considerable differences in this SPI within the Pacific region.

---

[44]   ILO. 2019. *Future of Work for Climate Resilience in the Pacific Islands*. Suva: ILO Office for Pacific Island Countries.
[45]   ADB. 2022. *Kiribati: Social Protection Indicator*. Manila.
[46]   ADB. 2022. *Cook Islands: Social Protection Indicator*. Manila.

Box 9: Social Services and Support for Older Persons in Palau

In 1976, assistance programs for older people from the Government of the United States were extended to Palau and included developing centers for social congregation, income generation, and hot lunches. The program was then assumed by the Government of Palau in 1999 under the Ministry of Community and Cultural Affairs. Today, senior centers serve hot lunches to persons ages 55 years and older residing in Koror and Airai, contain shops selling handicrafts made by seniors, and provide home lunch delivery to seniors residing in Koror who are medically certified as homebound. These services are not means-tested.

The government also allocates a small sum ($30,000 per year) to supplement the home care needs of older persons without income. This benefit takes the form of distribution of commodities purchased by the Ministry of Community and Cultural Affairs and delivered to eligible seniors once a year. Most outlying states also have senior centers, but these are used more for special events than as venues for daily activities or services. Finally, other home health services for the aged and people with disabilities are financed through the HealthCare Fund, with the premiums for seniors and the unemployed paid by the government.

Source: ADB. 2022. *Palau: Social Protection Indicator*. Manila.

Active LMPs comprise a variety of government-funded programs, including skills development and training, employment assistance, and cash- and food-for-work programs (see Box 10 for Samoa and Box 11 for the Marshall Islands for some examples). Some programs are little more than information sharing on employment opportunities, while others actively assist low-income rural residents to obtain seasonal agricultural work in Australia and New Zealand or provide material and market support to workers in remote communities, such as outer island copra producers. Alone, the amount of expenditure is a crude measure of the importance of these programs, as the per capita cost of these programs is not necessarily high.

Many Pacific DMCs have large youth populations with few opportunities for employment, especially for those who have not succeeded in school. Thus, many active LMPs are tailored to them. In PNG, for example, the Urban Youth Employment Project, which began in 2010, is funded by the World Bank and governments of Australia and PNG and has provided training in income generation, temporary employment, and incomes to more than 18,500 unemployed urban youth, 41% of them young women. The program also reduced anti-social behaviors and the crime rate.[47] Basic life skills and job readiness training has been provided to 6,700 youth to improve their transition into the formal or informal workplace—still small numbers in comparison to PNG's large population, however.[48] In Fiji, the National Employment Centre, established in 2009, has continued to expand its programs and to increase the number of participants, also aiming to assist disadvantaged young people in joining the formal workforce.

---

[47] O. Ivaschenko, D. Naidoo, D. Newhouse, and S. Sultan. 2017. Can Public Works Programs Reduce Youth Crime? Evidence from Papua New Guinea's Youth Employment Project. *IZA Journal of Development and Migration.* 7 (9).

[48] ADB. 2022. *Papua New Guinea: Social Protection Indicator*. Manila.

Box 10: Support to Formal Sector Employees in Samoa

In Samoa, two labor market programs are operated by the Ministry of Commerce, Industry and Labour:

Apprenticeship program. Mandated under the Apprenticeship Act (2014) and Apprenticeship Regulations (2015), this program enables young people to combine work and part-time study to gain trade qualifications. The Faculty of Applied Science at the National University of Samoa implements the formal training component, offering seven courses: motor mechanics, electrical, fitting and machinery, plumbing, carpentry and joinery, welding and fabrication, and refrigeration and air conditioning. The practical component requires students to seek employers, but the ministry can assist.

Employment services. The ministry also helps people seeking employment by providing skills training and finding job placements, particularly for applicants of the seasonal employment programs in New Zealand and Australia.

Source: ADB. 2022. *Samoa: Social Protection Indicator*. Manila.

Box 11: Skills Development Program in the Marshall Islands

The National Training Council provides an internship program for young jobseekers, particularly unemployed youth and secondary school or college graduates. The program aims to increase the skills and work ethic of participants and to better prepare them for employment in the Marshall Islands or overseas, helps connect jobseekers with employers, and conducts on-the-job training. A measure of success is if a graduating intern obtains paid work or returns to school. The program is funded through the General Non-Resident Worker's Fund and Supplemental Education.

Source: ADB. 2022. *Marshall Islands: Social Protection Indicator*. Manila.

Several governments assist in the training and recruitment of seasonal agriculture work abroad under the Australia's Seasonal Worker Programme and New Zealand's Recognised Seasonal Employer Scheme. Fiji, Kiribati, Nauru, PNG, Samoa, Solomon Islands, Tonga, Tuvalu, and Vanuatu have also signed on to the Pacific Australia Labour Mobility scheme, which enables Australian employers to recruit low-skilled and unskilled workers from Pacific islands on contracts of up to 3 years in sectors such as accommodation and food services; health care and social assistance; and nonseasonal agriculture, forestry, and fishing.

Fiji, Kiribati, the FSM, PNG, Samoa, Tuvalu, and Vanuatu have maritime training institutions that train residents—mostly men—to work on foreign merchant marine or fishing vessels. Box 12 discusses in more detail the Maritime Training in Kiribati. Remittances from these seafarers provide a significant part of the gross national product of these small countries.[49]

---

[49] R. Gillett. 2016. *Fisheries in the Economies of Pacific Island Countries and Territories*. Noumea: SPC. https:// www.spc.int/sites/default/files/wordpresscontent/wp-content/uploads/2016/11/Gillett_16_Benefish-fisheries-in-economies-of-pacific-countries.pdf.

Box 12: Maritime Training in Kiribati

Kiribati's Marine Training Centre (which merged with Kiribati's Fisheries Training Centre), trains locals as merchant seafarers to work in the international shipping and fishery industries. The center is government-funded and managed by the Ministry of Labour and Human Resource Development and supported by international donor agencies and maritime industry organizations. The center is the most important source of private sector employment for Kiribati, generating significant foreign exchange earnings through remittances of its graduates.

Located adjacent to the center, a German shipping recruitment agency, South Pacific Marine Services, also has helped trainees secure jobs. Its long-standing arrangement with the center and government however, ended in 2021 due to costs brought by the COVID-19 pandemic and failed attempts to negotiate for repatriation of seafarers stranded abroad due to pandemic-related travel restrictions.

Sources: R. Gillett. 2016. *Fisheries in the Economies of Pacific Island Countries and Territories.* Noumea: SPC. https://www.spc.int/sites/default/files/wordpresscontent/wp-content/uploads/2016/11/Gillett_16_Benefish-fisheries-in-economies-of-pacific-countries.pdf; M. Borovnik, C. Bedford, and R. Bailey. 2021. Has COVID-19 Ended Seafaring for Kiribati? *DevPolicyBlog.* Canberra: Australian National University Development Policy Centre. https://devpolicy.org/has-covid-19-ended-seafaring-for-kiribati-20211222/.

The informal sector accounts for a large part of employment in most Pacific DMCs and absorbs—or disguises—a significant degree of underemployment. In Solomon Islands, for example, about 85% of the working-age population is in the informal sector, and 95% of the rural population is considered subsistence producers.[50] Rural access to basic services is often limited, rural incomes are low, and the exposure of remote communities to climate-related shocks is high, all of which have long contributed to the movement of people from rural to urban areas. People often express preference for rural or village life, but the difficulty of sustaining livelihoods there can discourage them from staying or returning.

Kiribati, the FSM, and the Marshall Islands use controlled and subsidized copra prices to support outer island producers. Samoa also has several programs that support producers in the informal sector—particularly those that produce traditional goods—thereby helping maintain elements of Samoan culture. For example, a weaving program was initiated by the government through the Ministry of Women, Community and Social Development to support village-level women's committees and their weaving of Samoa's highly regarded traditional fine mats. The program provides an important source of income for women in the informal sector.[51] Similarly, in Tonga, various national informal sector producer associations have been established—including weavers, agriculture workers, and handicraft producers—through which training, marketing assistance, and other government and donor support are channeled. Associations of this kind have also recently been set up through pandemic recovery projects in Fiji, Palau, and Vanuatu.[52]

---

[50]   ILO. 2017. *A Study on the Future of Work in the Pacific.* Suva: ILO Office for Pacific Island Countries.
[51]   ADB. 2022. *Samoa: Social Protection Indicator.* Manila.
[52]   UNDP. 2020. Inclusive Economic Recovery through Sustainable Enterprises in the Informal Economies of Fiji, Palau, Tonga and Vanuatu. *Multi-Partner Trust Fund Office Gateway.* https://mptf.undp.org/factsheet/project/00124564.

As the COVID-19 pandemic took hold in 2020, many Pacific DMCs closed their borders; trade and tourism, in particular, were shuttered; and unemployment escalated. Box 13 discusses the social protection response to the COVID-19 pandemic in the Cook Islands. Chapter V of this report discusses in more detail the Pacific response to the pandemic, but the rapid response of several governments—to the employment crisis, of rolling out unemployment support, and holding back on job redundancies wherever possible—occurred. This begs the question as to why in normal times, unemployment and active LMPs attract relatively little investment compared with other aspects of social protection.

Box 13: Unemployment Relief in the COVID-19 Pandemic Response in the Cook Islands

The economic response plan to the COVID-19 pandemic in the Cook Islands was led by the Ministry of Finance and Economic Management, with other government agencies joining in its implementation. The Ministry of Internal Affairs used the existing social assistance system to rapidly roll out support for welfare recipients due to school closures. It also managed an unemployment benefit, employment services, and the Hardship Fund.

The Cook Islands National Superannuation Fund and Ministry of Finance and Economic Management managed the Wage Subsidy, an initiative that had the largest expenditure and most beneficiaries, reaching 3,500 people. The government also maintained the public servant payroll at full pay with no redundancies related to the pandemic.

Source: ADB. 2022. *Cook Islands: Social Protection Indicator*. Manila.

III. Social Protection Indicator Breadth, Depth, and Distributional Dimensions

Introduction

This chapter reports on the SPI breadth of coverage and depth of benefits in 2018. The SPI notes two kinds of beneficiaries: target (i.e., potential) and actual beneficiaries. The SPI breadth of coverage indicates how many (the proportion) of the target beneficiaries of social protection programs receive the benefits. The SPI depth of benefits indicates the average value, measured as a percentage of national GDP per capita, of the benefits that actual beneficiaries receive. The increased or decreased coverage of social protection programs and average value of benefits per beneficiary can demonstrate greater or less expenditure on programs, fewer or more beneficiaries, or both.

In this region, where most social protection coverage rates are low, any reduction in coverage is generally negative. The implications of a decrease in program depth are more ambiguous; a large drop in the average value of benefits per beneficiary can signal that more people are participating in these programs. This is occurring in PNG, where health insurance is now more widely available, and in Vanuatu, where the National Provident Fund now services informal sector workers.

The characteristics of beneficiaries are then examined, as is the extent to which government expenditure on social protection remedies essential social and economic inequalities—between the poor and the nonpoor, females and males, and people with disabilities and those without disabilities.

Breadth of Coverage

In 2018, the average SPI breadth of coverage in the Pacific region is 32.0%, but the only DMCs where this regional average reflects the national situation are the Cook Islands (36.6%), Nauru (36.9%), and Fiji (39.4%). Coverage is noted to be highest in Palau (113.3%), and lowest in Solomon Islands (3.0%) and PNG (1.3%) (Figure 8).

Note that coverage figures can exceed 100% where people are eligible for multiple types of benefits, as in Palau, where the superannuation scheme is supplemented by two health insurance programs that benefit almost the entire population. The SPI depth can exceed 100% where well-subscribed programs benefit a relatively small number of people, such as where the formal job sector is relatively small, as in Solomon Islands and PNG—and this determines eligibility for their national provident funds.

Figure 8: **Breadth of Coverage and Depth of Benefits by Country, 2018**

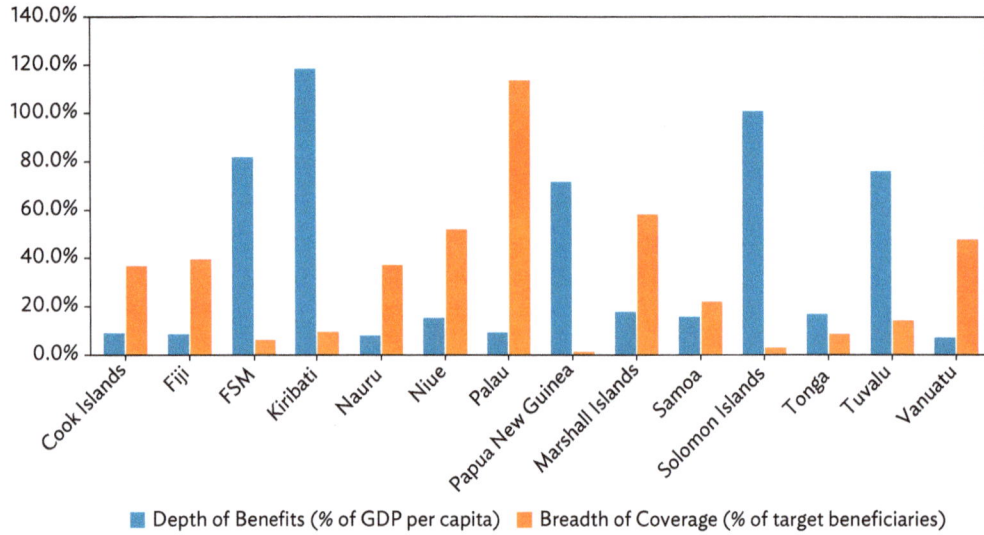

FSM = Federated States of Micronesia, GDP = gross domestic product.

Source: ADB estimates based on consultants' country reports.

Figure 8 suggests that where coverage is high, average benefits tend to be relatively small, as in the Cook Islands, Fiji, the Marshall Islands, Nauru, Palau, and Vanuatu. The opposite situation also holds—where average benefits are relatively large, coverage is generally low, as in Kiribati, the FSM, PNG, Solomon Islands, and Tuvalu. This pattern is more evident when the DMCs are grouped by their national income category, which suggests that coverage is high but with less depth of benefits in high-income countries; the opposite situation holds in lower-income countries (Figure 9).

Figure 9: **Depth of Benefits and Breadth of Coverage by Income Group, 2018**

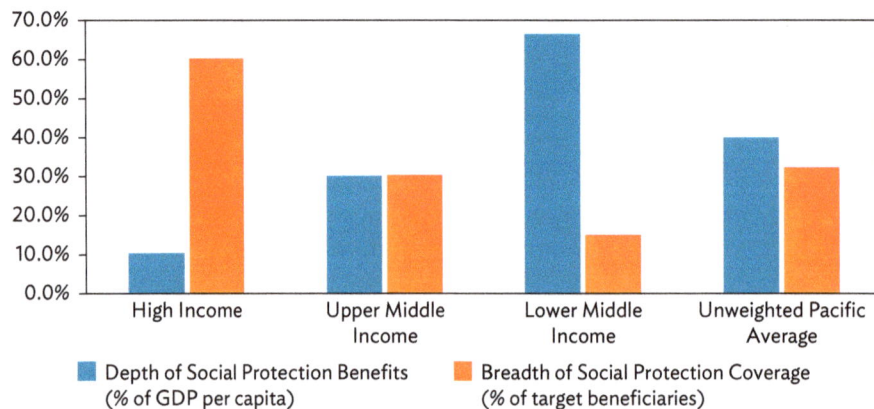

GDP = gross domestic product.

Source: ADB estimates based on consultants' country reports.

Such is the diversity of Pacific DMCs, however, that this neat picture dissolves when national situations are examined. Figure 10 demonstrates that there is more at play than national income in deciding the extent and types of social protection programs in each country.

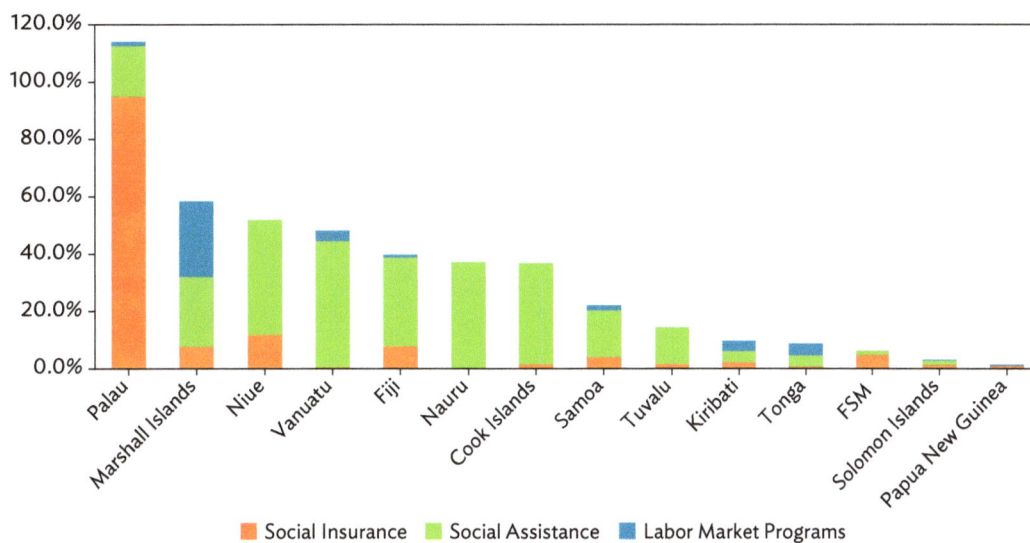

Figure 10: **Breadth of Coverage, Ordered, 2018** (% of **total** target beneficiaries)

FSM = Federated States of Micronesia.

Source: ADB estimates based on consultants' county reports.

Social protection program coverage levels are low or very low in most Pacific DMCs. In only three did at least half of all intended or potential beneficiaries receive benefits: Palau (113.3%), the Marshall Islands (58.0%), and Niue (51.8%). In the Cook Islands, Fiji, and Nauru, a little over 33.0% of potential beneficiaries actually benefit from social protection expenditures; in Samoa, the coverage rate averages 21.8%. In the other five DMCs, less than 15.0% of potential beneficiaries receive benefits: Tuvalu (14.2%), Kiribati (9.4%), Tonga (8.6%), the FSM (6.1%), Solomon Islands (3.0%), and PNG (1.3%). Where figures reach more than 100.0% (e.g., Palau), the distribution of benefits is concentrated on some groups in the population, i.e., they receive benefits from more than one social protection program. By program category, the average coverage rates are highest for social assistance and lowest for active LMPs (Table 6).

The regional average coverage for social insurance is pulled up by Palau's high figure. Leaving Palau out of the calculation, the regional average drops to 2.6%, a more realistic indicator of the narrow coverage of social insurance programs—principally provident funds—in most Pacific DMCs.

Table 6: **Breadth of Coverage by Category, 2018**

(% of total target beneficiaries)

	Overall Breadth of Coverage	Social Insurance	Social Assistance	Labor Market Programs
Palau	113.3	94.3	17.5	1.5
Marshall Islands	58.0	7.6	24.2	26.2
Niue	51.6	11.7	39.8	...
Vanuatu	47.6	0.5	43.7	3.5
Fiji	39.4	7.7	30.9	0.8
Nauru	36.9	0.3	36.6	...
Cook Islands	36.6	1.4	35.2	...
Samoa	21.8	3.9	16.2	1.7
Tuvalu	14.2	1.6	12.6	...
Kiribati	9.4	2.1	3.9	3.4
Tonga	8.6	0.7	3.9	4.0
FSM	6.1	4.7	1.4	...
Solomon Islands	3.0	1.2	1.6	0.2
Papua New Guinea	1.3	1.0	...	0.2

... = no data, FSM = Federated States of Micronesia.

Source: ADB estimates based on consultants' country reports.

Depth of Benefits

The depth of benefits is measured by dividing the social protection expenditure by the number of actual beneficiaries of social protection and is expressed in terms of GDP per capita. The depth of social protection programs is influenced most by social insurance, with relatively large benefit amounts going to small groups of people as monthly pensions or lump-sum payments upon retirement. Social insurance benefits are well above the GDP per capita in DMCs with low rates of formal employment and low levels of GDP per capita, i.e., Solomon Islands (242.1%), Vanuatu (189.2%), Kiribati (180.4%), Tonga (136.1%), and the Marshall Islands (108.7%) (Table 7). The opposite pattern holds for social assistance benefits. In most DMCs, they average less than 10.0% of GDP per capita but are higher in Tuvalu, Kiribati, the FSM, and Solomon Islands.

Dimensions of Social Protection

Given the prevalence of poverty and the manifold disadvantages faced by females and people with disabilities in the Pacific region, it can be assumed that expenditures on social protection programs principally assist the most disadvantaged and

Table 7: **Depth of Benefits by Category, 2018**
(% of **GDP** per capita)

Country	Overall	Social Insurance	Social Assistance	Labor Market Programs
Palau	5.6	5.5	6.3	5.3
Nauru	7.9	41.3	7.6	0.0
Vanuatu	7.2	189.2	5.7	0.9
Fiji	8.5	29.0	3.4	7.2
Cook Islands	8.9	33.0	8.0	0.0
Niue	15.1	26.9	2.2	0.0
Samoa	15.7	62.5	5.8	2.5
Tonga	16.9	136.1	10.0	1.4
Marshall Islands	17.7	108.7	3.7	4.2
Tuvalu	55.5	11.7	55.7	0.0
Papua New Guinea	71.4	86.6	0.0	4.0
FSM	81.6	89.6	54.5	0.0
Kiribati	118.1	180.4	22.6	189.3
Solomon Islands	165.2	242.1	194.0	7.9
Pacific Average	**39.6**	**103.7**	**14.3**	**17.5**

FSM = Federated States of Micronesia, GDP = gross domestic product.

Source: ADB estimates based on consultants' country reports.

vulnerable—but this is generally not so, due to the dominance of social insurance. As social insurance programs are mostly self-funded, they benefit those who contribute the most funds. This section examines the ways in which benefits of social protection programs are distributed and the characteristics of the main beneficiaries.

1.   Disaggregation by Poverty Status

Recent surveys and other research have found high poverty rates in most Pacific DMCs. Pacific island societies value traditions of wealth distribution and mutual support within families and communities, but these support mechanisms have been weakened by economic and social changes. While extreme poverty is not prevalent in the region, in Fiji, the FSM, the Marshall Islands, and PNG, over one-third of all households fall below national basic needs poverty lines, meaning that they cannot maintain the most basic standards of living considered adequate in their country (Table 8).

In Fiji, for example, the World Bank estimated that 2.3% of the population lives in extreme poverty, 2.5% of the population lives below the national food poverty line, and 34.0% of the population lives below the basic needs poverty line.[53] Increasingly, Pacific island governments acknowledge that family, community, and other informal

---

[53]   World Bank. 2017. *Systematic Country Diagnostic 2017: Republic of Fiji.* Washington, DC.

Table 8: Population Living below National Basic Needs
Poverty Lines, 2018

Country	Population ('000)	Poor ('000)	Share of Poor (%)
FSM	104.3	42.8	41.0
Papua New Guinea	9,017.9	3,433.9	38.1
Marshall Islands	54.6	20.0	36.6
Fiji	888.4	302.1	34.0
Tonga	100.1	27.2	27.2
Tuvalu	10.5	2.8	27.0
Nauru	11.4	2.7	24.0
Niue	1.8	0.1	4.8
Palau	17.5	3.4	19.4
Samoa	199.2	37.5	18.8
Kiribati	120.1	20.5	17.1
Solomon Islands	682.5	84.7	12.7
Vanuatu	304.5	35.5	12.5
Cook Islands	15.2	1.3	8.2

FSM = Federated States of Micronesia.

Note: As poverty is defined separately in each country (usually as relative—not absolute—poverty), the percentage shares of the poor are not directly comparable across countries.

Source: ADB estimates based on consultants' country reports.

support networks must be supplemented with strong, formal, state-led social programs, with growing support for the concept of a universal social floor.[54]

Information from the latest available household income and expenditure surveys (HIESs) or other poverty studies, administrative records, and estimates by government officials and ADB helped calculate the poverty-targeting rate of social protection programs in each DMC, a disaggregation of the SPI between the poor and nonpoor (Figure 11). Where program data were not available, it is assumed that (i) if a program is exclusively targeted at identifiable groups of poor, then 100% of the beneficiaries are poor; and (ii) if a program is not specifically for the poor, the national poverty incidence rate serves as a proxy for the proportion of beneficiaries who are poor.

In 2018, the SPI for the poor is greater than the SPI for the nonpoor only in Kiribati, reflecting its investment in supporting informal sector producers. In the Marshall Islands, Palau, and Solomon Islands particularly, the SPIs for the nonpoor are much greater than those for the poor, signaling the dominance of social insurance programs that provide most benefits to formal sector workers.

Figure 11: Disaggregation by Poverty Status, 2018

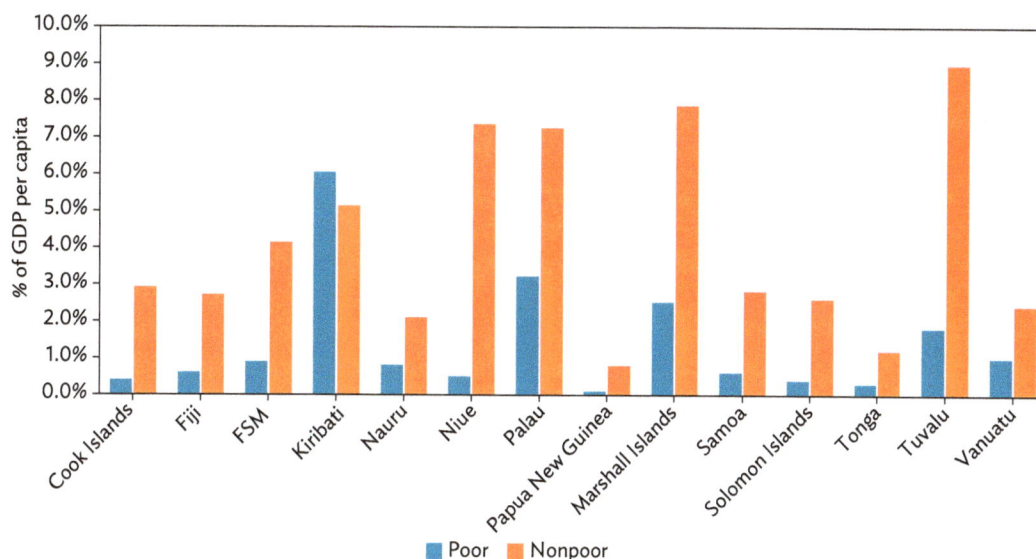

FSM = Federated States of Micronesia, GDP = gross domestic product.

Source: ADB estimates based on consultants' country reports.

2.   Disaggregation by Sex

The SPI is also disaggregated for women and men using the records of relevant agencies where sex-disaggregated data were available, census data when programs are provided equally for women and men, and other data sources where available.

Over the past several decades, Pacific island governments have made commitments to a series of international and regional conventions, declarations, and frameworks to advance gender equality and to promote women's empowerment, and there is movement almost everywhere toward creating more equal opportunities for women and men. Nonetheless, sharp inequalities remain—in the power men and women exercise at home, in the workplace, and in politics—and more so in DMCs with lower levels of human development.[55] Of all DMCs in the region for which the Gender Inequality Index was calculated in 2019, PNG has the lowest score of 0.725 and a ranking of 161 out of 162 in the global index. Fiji, the best-scoring Pacific DMC, is ranked only 78th globally.[56]

Men benefit most from contributory social insurance in the Pacific region for two reasons: (i) formal sector labor force participation is, on average, nearly 20 percentage points higher for men than women; and (ii) men have, on average, higher rates of pay. A good part of women's work in the household, community,

---

[55]   UNDP. 2019. *Human Development Report 2019—Beyond Income, Beyond Averages, Beyond Today: Inequalities in Human Development in the 21st Century.* New York; and E. Boccuzzi. 2021. *The Future of Work for Women in the Pacific Islands.* New York: The Asia Foundation.

[56]   UNDP. 2019. *Human Development Report 2019—Beyond Income, Beyond Averages, Beyond Today: Inequalities in Human Development in the 21st Century.* New York.

and informal sector goes unrecognized and undervalued, both in society and in official statistics. Many Pacific DMCs also have among the lowest levels in the region of female political participation. Moreover, Pacific DMCs have some of the highest rates of domestic violence in the world, with an estimated 63% of women in Melanesia, 44% in Micronesia, and 43% in Polynesia having experienced sexual violence by their intimate partners (footnote 56).

While some social assistance programs across the region aim to redress gender inequalities, particularly those suffered by poor households headed by women, most social protection benefits still accrue to men, because of the dominance of social insurance.

Figure 12 disaggregates the SPIs for women and for men by DMC. These are quite equal in Palau, the Cook Islands, and Samoa, but the SPIs for men well outstrip those for women in Fiji, Kiribati, PNG, Solomon Islands, and Vanuatu. In Fiji, men are also the main beneficiaries of the new, well-endowed Ex-Servicemen's After Care Fund. While women were the main beneficiaries under the previous social assistance program, men now can obtain more social assistance than they once did from the universal benefit programs.

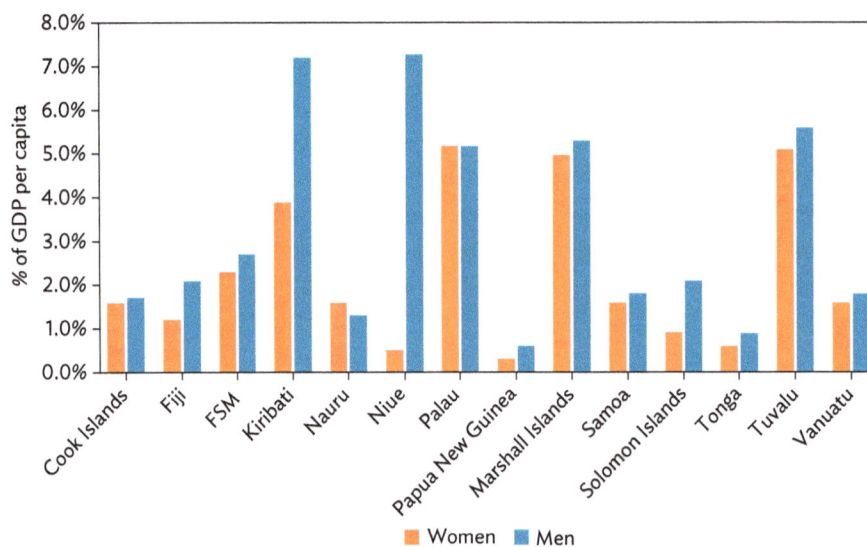

Figure 12: **Disaggregation by Sex, 2018**

FSM = Federated States of Micronesia, GDP = gross domestic product.

Source: ADB estimates based on consultants' country reports.

3.   Disaggregation by Disability Status

Many DMCs have long provided some type of paid benefits to children or adults with disabilities, albeit often inadequate benefits available only to the most disadvantaged in this group. Since ratification of the CRPD in 2015, several Pacific DMCs have implemented larger programs of assistance, however.

This is the first time that the SPI has been disaggregated for people with and without disabilities; therefore, no time series is possible. It is straightforward to measure participation in targeted disability programs, but it is difficult to assess the participation of people with disabilities in more general social protection programs. The estimates used in this report thus assume that the proportion of beneficiaries who receive general benefits mirrors the proportion of people with disabilities in the overall population or the population of a particular cohort (e.g., older persons). This is a necessary assumption but by no means necessarily true. In most DMCs, there is also some form of government registration or medical screening process to confirm their eligibility for various programs, which may be discriminatory in some respects.

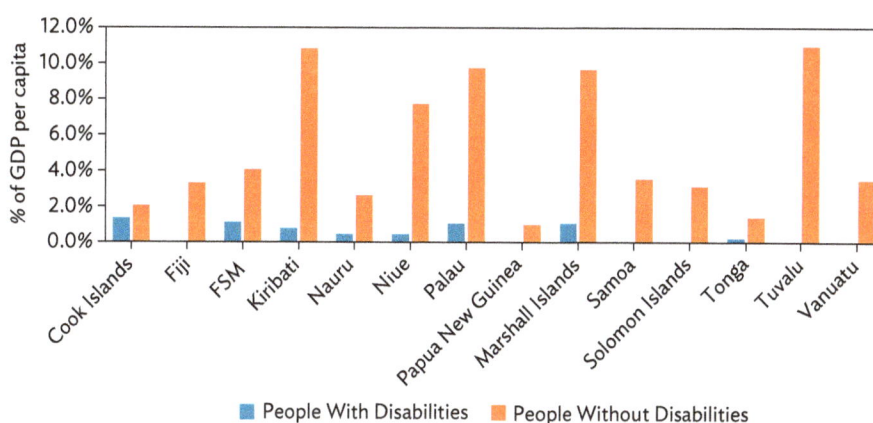

Figure 13: **Disaggregation by Disability Status, 2018**

FSM = Federated States of Micronesia, GDP = gross domestic product.

Source: ADB estimates based on consultants' country reports.

The SPIs for people without disabilities far exceed the SPIs for people with disabilities in every Pacific DMC (Figure 13). The best situations are in the Cook Islands, Kiribati, the Marshall Islands, the FSM, and Palau (presented in Box 14). Other than CSO-, NGO- or church-supported programs, disability programs in the Marshall Islands, the FSM, and Palau are partially funded under US federal government programs and follow the eligibility criteria set by these programs. Like Palau, the Special Education Fund in the Marshall Islands and the FSM cater to children with disabilities, and the respective national superannuation schemes are only for adults who were in paid employment when they became disabled.[57] Despite the relatively better situations for people with disabilities in these Pacific DMCs, many remain underserved.

---

[57] The FSM Social Security Administration further requires that all applicants for the disability benefit be fully insured with at least $1,500 in contributions. ADB. 2022. *Republic of the Marshall Islands: Social Protection Indicator.* Manila; and ADB. 2022. *Federated States of Micronesia: Social Protection Indicator.* Manila.

Box 14: People with Disabilities in Palau's Social Protection Program

Palau has one of the most comprehensive social protection systems in the Pacific. Complementing the support provided to most older people through Palau's traditional family system, comprehensive provisions for aged pensions and other social assistance payments are funded by the Government of Palau or the Government of the United States. As well as high expenditure on public health services, there is a minimum wage; subsidized public utilities; and other services for low-income families, the older population, and people with disabilities.

Services for vulnerable populations rely heavily on United States federal government program funding. These programs principally aid children and at-risk adolescents, with little funding allocated for other vulnerable groups, including adults with disabilities. Despite the services and small government stipends provided for adults with disabilities, a 2017 study found that people with disabilities remain disadvantaged in regard to education, employment, and poverty status.

Sources: Government of Palau. 2019. *Pathway to 2030: Progressing with Our Past toward a Resilient, Sustainable and Equitable Future.* Ngerulmud; Government of Palau, Office of Planning and Statistics and UNDP. 2017. *Palau: Analysis of the 2014 Household Income and Expenditure Survey: Report on the Estimation of Basic Needs Poverty Lines and the Incidence and Characteristics of Hardship and Basic Needs Poverty in Palau.* Ngerulmud; UNICEF Pacific, Office of Planning and Statistics and The Pacific Community. 2017. *Palau Disability Report: An Analysis of 2015 Census of Population, Housing and Agriculture.* Suva: UNICEF Pacific.

Patterns of Change, 2009–2018

1.   Countries in this Analysis

In 2009, when this series of Pacific SPI reports began, only eight DMCs were covered: Fiji, the Marshall Islands, Nauru, Palau, PNG, Samoa, Solomon Islands, and Vanuatu. In 2012, four DMCs were added: the Cook Islands, the FSM, Kiribati, and Tonga. In this 2018 report, the remaining two DMCs in the region are included: Niue and Tuvalu. The changing pattern of inclusion creates some difficulty in charting patterns of change. In this section, therefore, only DMCs for which there are data from 2009 are included. Note that the averages cited here refer only to the first eight DMCs; therefore, they may not be consistent with figures cited in the previous discussion.

The average SPI for the Pacific region has grown from 3.06% of GDP per capita in 2009 to 4.70% in 2018, with the steepest rise occurring between 2012 and 2015.[58] For the most part, DMCs with a higher SPI in 2009 have a higher SPI in 2018—although Fiji bucks this trend with a falling SPI, as does Solomon Islands with a considerable rise in its SPI. PNG and Vanuatu had the lowest SPIs in 2009, as they do in 2018 (Table 9).

2.   Social Insurance

Overall, while the average SPI for the Pacific region steadily increased over the past decade, social insurance remains the largest component in the SPI, rising from 2.4% of GDP per capita in 2009 to 2.8% in 2012, 3.3% in 2015, and slightly increasing to 3.4% in 2018 (Table 10 and Figure 14). However as a proportion of the SPI, the share

Table 9: Progress in Social Protection Indicator by Country, 2009 to 2018
(% of GDP per capita)

Country	2009	2012	2015	2018
Palau	7.7	7.7	8.5	10.4
Fiji	6.2	4.5	3.3	3.3
Marshall Islands	4.7	7.7	10.6	10.3
Samoa	2.8	2.7	3.3	3.4
Solomon Islands	1.0	1.4	3.4	3.0
Nauru	0.9	0.7	4.3	2.9
Papua New Guinea	0.6	0.8	0.8	0.9
Vanuatu	0.6	0.8	1.4	3.4
Unweighted Pacific Average	**3.1**	**3.3**	**4.4**	**4.7**

GDP = gross domestic product.

Note: The averages are computed for countries with complete data from 2009 to 2018; therefore, the 2018 average may differ from this data table.

Source: ADB estimates based on consultants' country reports.

Table 10: Social Insurance Contribution to Social Protection Indicator by Country, 2009–2018
(% of GDP per capita)

Country	2009	2012	2015	2018
Palau	6.7	7.4	8.0	9.2
Fiji	5.5	3.9	2.8	2.2
Marshall Islands	3.0	6.4	9.0	8.3
Samoa	1.7	1.7	2.2	2.4
Solomon Islands	1.0	1.3	2.8	2.9
Papua New Guinea	0.6	0.8	0.7	0.9
Vanuatu	0.4	0.8	1.2	0.9
Nauru	0.3	0.1	0.1	0.1
Unweighted Pacific Average	**2.4**	**2.8**	**3.3**	**3.4**

GDP = gross domestic product.

Note: The averages are computed for countries with complete data from 2009 to 2018; therefore, the 2018 average may differ from this data table.

Source: ADB estimates based on consultants' country reports.

of social insurance has declined from over three-quarters in 2009 to just over 70% in 2018. This reflects the increased expenditure on the other two categories of social protection, particularly social assistance over the period.

Social insurance continues to contribute the most to the SPI in each DMC. It has been consistently the highest in Palau, has seen the greatest gain in the Marshall Islands, but

Figure 14: Overall Social Protection Indicator and Social Protection Indicator for Social Insurance, 2009–2018

(% of GDP per capita)

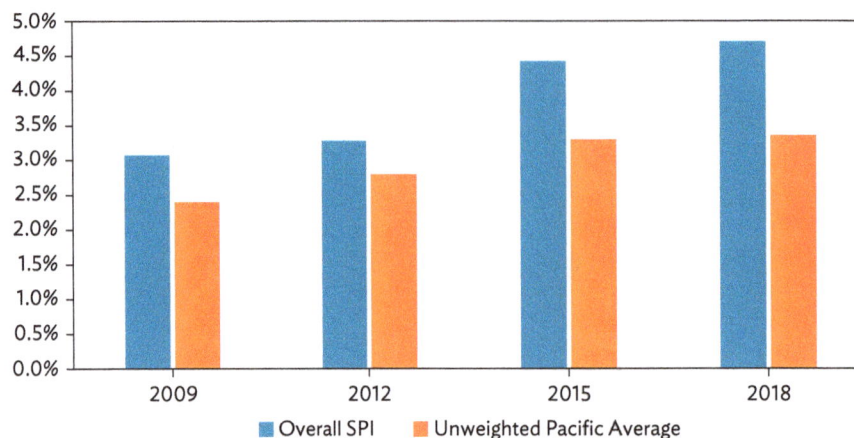

■ Overall SPI   ■ Unweighted Pacific Average

GDP = gross domestic produc, SPI = Social Protection Indicator.

Source: ADB estimates based on consultants' country reports.

has more than halved in Fiji since 2009. One reason for its persistent dominance is the large sums of money created through contributory retirement benefit programs as well as increased health insurance. The main reason for the slight decline of the overall share of social insurance in the regional SPI has been increased national investment in social assistance programs.

Contributory health insurance programs are becoming more common, some operated by private companies and catering to people who can afford the premiums—mostly those in formal employment. In PNG, for example, Nambawan Super Limited and NasFund are contributory schemes for health and unemployment insurance. Others are an amalgam of public and private investments. In addition to the Civil Service Pension Trust Fund, Palau has two health insurance schemes that have operated since 2010 through the HealthCare Fund: individual medical savings accounts and National Health Insurance, a pooled universal social health insurance fund. These are funded through mandatory contributions of 2.5% of earned incomes, and together cover almost the whole population. The government pays subsidized contributions for citizens who are over age 60 years and not working, and for people with disabilities who are not working.[59]

3.   Social Assistance

As an average across the region, the SPI for social assistance has risen overall, although it declined from 0.6% in 2009 to 0.4% in 2012, it rose to 0.9% in 2015 and 1.2% in 2018 (Table 11 and Figure 15). This reflects the growing value of individual benefits as well as greater investment in a larger number of programs. These programs

[59]   Palau Social Security Administration. http://ropssa.pw/.

are more often providing universal benefits to broadly defined vulnerable groups, such as the older population or all schoolchildren.

In 2009, the share of social assistance to the national SPI was the highest in the Marshall Islands, but has declined since. The greatest gains are in Nauru and Vanuatu, DMCs with low scores in 2009. PNG still does not have any social assistance programs.

Table 11: Social Assistance Contribution to Social Protection Indicator by Country, 2009–2018

(% of GDP per capita)

Country	2009	2012	2015	2018
Marshall Islands	1.2	0.8	0.8	0.9
Samoa	1.0	1.0	1.0	0.9
Palau	1.0	0.3	0.5	1.0
Fiji	0.6	0.5	0.5	1.1
Nauru	0.6	0.6	4.3	2.8
Vanuatu	0.3	0.0	0.4	2.5
Solomon Islands	0.0	0.0	0.0	0.0
Papua New Guinea	0.0	0.0	0.0	0.0
Unweighted Pacific Average	0.6	0.4	0.9	1.2

0.0 = value less than 0.1 or no data, GDP = gross domestic product.

Note: The averages are computed for countries with complete data from 2009 to 2018; therefore, the 2018 average may differ from this data table.

Source: ADB estimates based on consultants' country reports.

Figure 15: Overall Social Protection Indicator and Social Protection Indicator for Social Assistance, 2009–2018

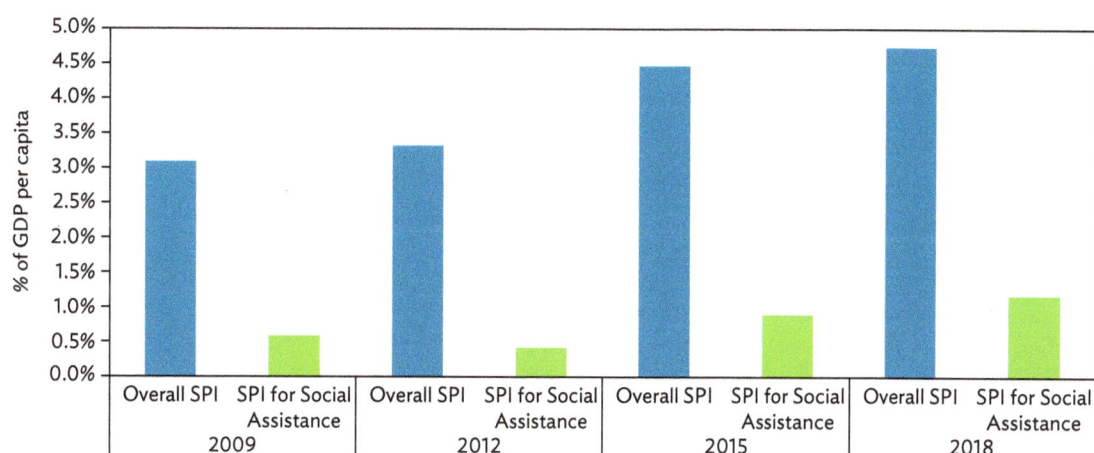

GDP = gross domestic product, SPI = Social Protection Indicator.

Source: ADB estimates based on consultants' country reports.

4. Labor Market Programs

While the average SPI for the Pacific region has steadily increased, expenditure on active LMPs remains miniscule, despite its increase from 0.1% of GDP per capita in 2009 to 0.2% in 2015 and 2018 (Table 12 and Figure 16).

Table 12: Labor Market Program Contribution to Social Protection Indicator by Country, 2009–2018

(% of GDP per capita)

Country	2009	2012	2015	2018
Marshall Islands	0.60	0.50	0.80	1.10
Solomon Islands	0.02	0.10	0.60	0.10
Samoa	0.00	0.03	0.10	0.10
Fiji	0.00	0.00	0.00	0.10
Palau	0.00	0.00	0.00	0.20
Vanuatu	0.00	0.00	0.00	0.00
Papua New Guinea	0.00	0.00	0.00	0.00
Nauru	0.00	0.00	0.00	0.00
Unweighted Pacific Average	0.10	0.10	0.20	0.20

0.0 = value less than 0.1 or no data, GDP = gross domestic product.

Note: The averages are computed for countries with complete data from 2009 to 2018; therefore, the 2018 average may differ from this data table.

Source: ADB estimates based on consultants' country reports.

Figure 16: Overall Social Protection Indicator and Social Protection Indicator for Labor Market Programs, 2009–2018

(% of GDP per capita)

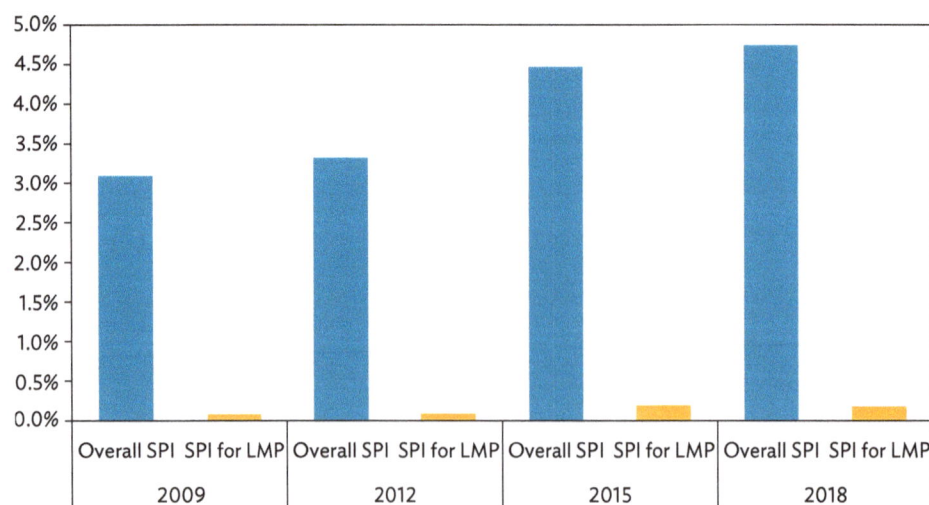

GDP = gross domestic product, LMP = labor market program, SPI = Social Protection Indicator.

Source: ADB estimates based on consultants' country reports.

As mentioned previously, expenditure alone is not the best measure of the significance of these programs, as targeted training and job placement activities generally cost much less than programs that distribute cash benefits. There are concerns about the quality and relevance of some active LMPs, however; for example, many vocational and technical training programs do not match local skilled employment needs, because industry associations and employers are not involved in developing their curricula.[60]

Meanwhile, some active LMPs that were once successful have been underfunded or disbanded, such as a national job training program along with trade schools and programs (e.g., the Pohnpei Agriculture and Trade School) in the FSM.[61] Nonetheless, the returns from investments in greater employment generation are being realized in some DMCs, either by expanding local employment and self-employment opportunities or building on existing patterns of population mobility to facilitate work overseas and the return of newly skilled people, remittances, and savings.

Although not included in this section, Kiribati stands out as investing the most in employment support and growth since 2015. Over the past decade, a large share of Kiribati's national income has come from fishing licenses—amounting to almost 72% of national income in 2018—and the government has thus invested more heavily in social protection.

In 2016, the government doubled the market price for copra, substantially increasing income support for outer island producers through its Copra Subsidy Scheme. While the copra industry provides the economic and social backbone of the nation and there is a case for support of the industry through price subsidies, administrative costs of the program are high. There is a need to improve the efficiency and administration of the industry and to ensure that the support package is fiscally sustainable.[62]

The government has also facilitated a large increase in the number of people participating in the seasonal worker programs operated by New Zealand and Australia. Kiribati's SPI for labor market programs is 6.5% in 2018, up from 3.6% in 2015.[63]

5.   Breadth of Coverage

Table 13 shows how the SPI breadth has changed in the various DMCs from 2009 to 2018. Palau saw the largest increase. There are also notable gains in Vanuatu, Nauru, the Marshall Islands, and Fiji. In Palau, the Marshall Islands, and Vanuatu, these are mostly due to expanded social insurance programs; in Fiji and Nauru, these are mostly reflected by new social assistance programs.

---

[60]   ILO. 2017. *A Study on the Future of Work in the Pacific.* Suva: ILO Office for Pacific Island Countries.
[61]   ADB. 2022. *Federated States of Micronesia: Social Protection Indicator.* Manila.
[62]   World Bank. 2022. Review of Government of Kiribati Copra Subsidy Scheme. Washington, DC. Draft.
[63]   ADB. 2022. *Kiribati: Social Protection Indicator.* Manila.

Table 13: **Change to Overall Breadth by Country, 2009–2018**

(% of potential/targeted beneficiaries actually receiving benefits)

Country	2009	2012	2015	2018	2009–2018
Palau	29.9	108.0	97.3	133.3	83.4
Vanuatu	4.0	17.6	26.6	47.6	43.6
Nauru	5.8	6.7	37.1	36.9	31.1
Marshall Islands	26.9	21.3	22.5	58.0	31.0
Fiji	11.5	14.6	27.3	39.4	27.9
Solomon Islands	1.4	2.7	2.8	3.0	1.6
Papua New Guinea	0.1	0.2	0.3	1.3	1.1
Samoa	39.6	45.4	45.9	21.8	(17.8)

( ) = negative.

Source: ADB estimates based on consultants' country reports.

6.   Depth of Benefits

The depth of social protection programs has changed in the various DMCs between 2009 and 2018 (Table 14). Gains in depth are recorded in Solomon Islands, Samoa, and—to a small extent—the Marshall Islands. In both Solomon Islands and Samoa, this reflects greater per capita benefits from social assistance programs, and in Solomon Islands alone, also from active LMPs. The depth of social protection programs decreased in Nauru, Vanuatu, Palau, Fiji, and, most notably, PNG. In most DMCs, this situation demonstrates a larger range of social assistance programs with more widely distributed benefits.

Table 14: **Change to the Depth of Programs by Country, 2009–2018**

(% of GDP per capita)

Country	2009	2012	2015	2018	2009–2018
Solomon Islands	68.0	53.6	124.1	100.5	32.5
Samoa	7.0	5.9	7.1	15.7	8.6
Marshall Islands	17.6	36.0	47.2	17.7	0.1
Nauru	14.8	11.0	11.7	7.9	(6.8)
Vanuatu	15.3	4.8	4.9	7.2	(8.1)
Palau	25.7	7.2	8.8	9.2	(16.5)
Fiji	53.8	30.6	12.1	8.5	(45.3)
Papua New Guinea	516.1	503.5	189.2	71.4	(444.7)

( ) = negative, GDP = gross domestic product.

Source: ADB estimates based on consultants' country reports.

In 2018, the average depth of programs in the Pacific region is less than in 2015. Again, these figures differ among the three program categories. Social insurance seems to provide the highest average benefits but lower than in 2015. Social assistance programs have more beneficiaries who receive smaller benefits, also a significant decrease from 2015. The average benefits are lowest of all for active LMPs, again a decrease from 2015 (Figure 17).

Figure 17: **Depth of Benefits and Breadth of Coverage by Category, 2009–2018**

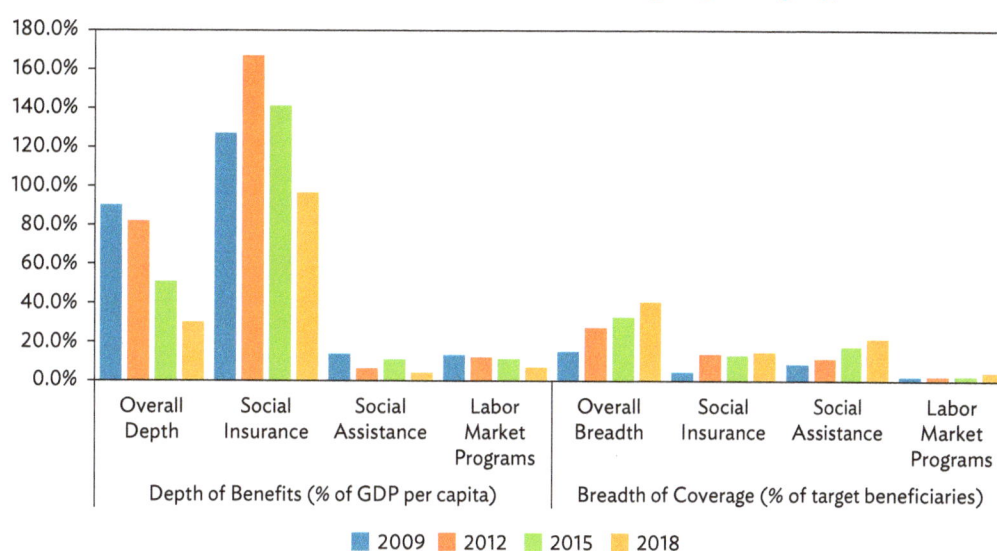

GDP = gross domestic product.

Source: ADB estimates based on consultants' country reports.

7.   Poverty Dimension

Table 15 tracks changes in the distribution of benefits to the poor and nonpoor from 2009 to 2018. It shows an unchanged situation in Solomon Islands, and a swing toward more support for the poor in Kiribati, Nauru, Palau, the Marshall Islands, Samoa, Tonga, and Vanuatu. In PNG and Fiji, however, the swing has been in the opposite direction, providing relatively more support to the nonpoor. Emphasis on the nonpoor shows the dominance of social insurance programs that provide most benefits to formal sector workers.

The share of social protection benefits going to the poor decreased in Fiji, as it expanded some universal social assistance programs. The share of social protection benefits going to the poor grew in Palau, the Marshall Islands, Nauru, Solomon Islands, and Vanuatu. In all DMCs, however, the greatest social protection benefits still accrue to the nonpoor, particularly so in PNG and even overall in the Marshall Islands, Nauru, Palau, and Solomon Islands.

Table 15: Change in the Social Protection Indicator for the Poor and the Nonpoor, 2009–2018 (%)

Country	2009		2012		2015		2018		Overall Change, 2009–2018	
	Poor	Nonpoor	Poor	Nonpoor	Poor	Nonpoor	Poor	Nonpoor	Poor	Nonpoor
Palau	0.4	7.3	1.1	6.6	1.3	7.3	1.9	7.7	1.6	0.3
Marshall Islands	1.0	3.7	1.7	5.9	2.4	8.2	2.5	7.8	1.4	4.1
Vanuatu	0.2	0.4	0.1	0.7	0.2	1.2	1.0	2.4	0.8	2.0
Nauru	0.3	0.6	0.2	0.6	1.1	3.3	0.8	2.1	0.5	1.5
Solomon Islands	0.0	1.0	0.1	1.4	0.8	2.7	0.4	2.6	0.4	1.6
Samoa	0.4	2.4	0.4	2.3	0.5	2.8	0.6	2.8	0.2	0.4
Papua New Guinea	0.1	0.5	0.1	0.7	0.1	0.6	0.1	0.8	0.0	0.3
Fiji	2.2	4.0	1.7	2.8	1.7	1.6	0.6	2.8	(1.7)	(1.3)

( ) = negative.

Source: ADB estimates based on consultants' country reports.

8. Sex Distribution

In 2009 and 2012, a gender difference—more precisely, an advantage to men—is evident in all Pacific DMCs (Table 16). This again reflects the dominance of social insurance in social protection expenditure, principally benefiting formal sector workers. Throughout the Pacific region, men have the largest share of formal sector jobs and, on average, higher rates of pay than women, providing men greater returns from contributory social insurance funds.[64]

However, in 2018, the difference between social protection benefits for women and men has narrowed in all DMCs, with Solomon Islands, Vanuatu, PNG, and Fiji still requiring further effort. Among eight countries with comparable data, seven countries increased their spending for women between 2009 and 2018 (Table 16). It is difficult to generalize among different national situations with various levels of social protection, but the largest gaps still reflect returns from social insurance programs. Where gaps have narrowed, this generally demonstrates wider access to social assistance, as in Fiji, and the implementation of universal pensions and other programs for older people, which benefit older women more due to longer female life expectancy.

---

[64]   In Kiribati, a country not included in the analysis, the gender difference is more indicative of the active LMPs that cater to seafarer training and employment, principally for men.

Table 16: **Change in the Social Protection Indicator for Women and Men, 2009–2018**
(%)

Country	2009		2012		2015		2018		Overall Change, 2009–2018	
	Women	Men	Women	Men	Women	Men	Women	Men	Women	Men
Marshall Islands	1.6	3.1	2.1	5.5	3.0	7.6	5.0	5.3	3.3	2.2
Solomon Islands	0.3	0.7	0.1	1.3	1.1	2.3	0.9	2.1	0.6	1.4
Palau	2.7	5.0	3.3	4.5	3.6	4.9	5.2	5.2	2.5	0.2
Nauru	0.4	0.5	0.3	0.4	2.3	2.0	1.6	1.3	1.2	0.8
Vanuatu	0.2	0.4	0.3	0.5	0.5	0.9	1.6	1.8	1.4	1.4
Samoa	1.3	1.5	1.2	1.5	1.5	1.8	1.6	1.8	0.3	0.3
Papua New Guinea	0.2	0.4	0.3	0.5	0.3	0.6	0.3	0.6	0.1	0.2
Fiji	1.7	4.5	1.6	2.9	1.3	2.0	1.2	2.1	(0.5)	(2.4)

( ) = negative.

Source: ADB estimates based on consultants' country reports.

Conclusion

From 2009 to 2018, the SPIs of the Pacific region steadily rose, with a small—but significant—redirection of social protection expenditure. The proportion going to social insurance slightly declined, and that going toward a more diverse pool of social assistance programs has grown. The SPIs for active LMPs doubled but from a tiny base, keeping this third category a mere fraction of the size of the other two (Figures 18 and 19). These regional figures, however, cloak a diversity of policies and programs among the eight DMCs.

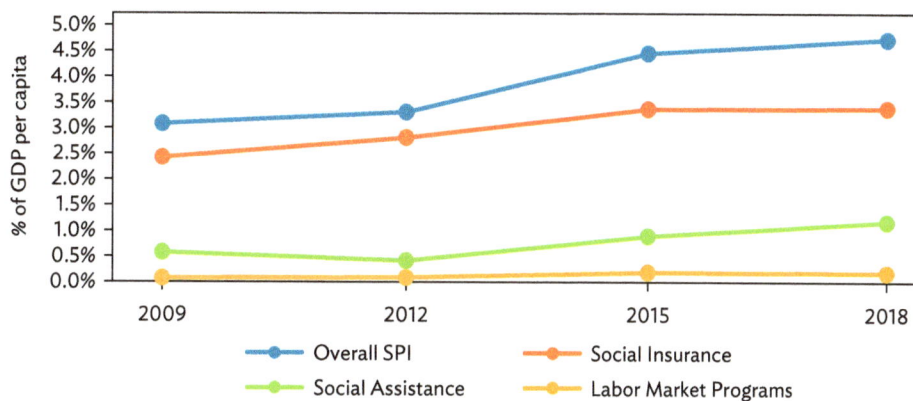

Figure 18: **Overall Increase in Social Protection Indicators in the Pacific, 2009–2018**

GDP = gross domestic product, SPI = Social Protection Indicator.

Source: ADB estimates based on consultants' country reports.

Figure 19: Progress in Social Protection by Category, 2009–2018

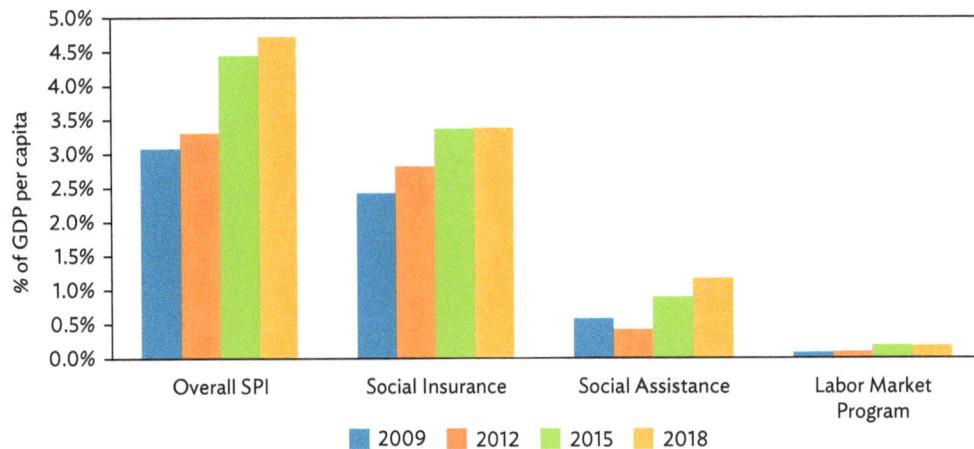

GDP = gross domestic product, SPI = Social Protection Indicator.

Source: ADB estimates based on consultants' country reports.

Although changes to regional and national investments in social protection are small, they are significant, indicating greater awareness by governments of long-standing patterns of unequal development and more focused commitments to redress inequality. The SPI for active LMPs indicates that these programs remain relatively underfunded and underdeveloped. The COVID-19 pandemic has underscored the importance of finding sustainable employment and self-employment opportunities in all Pacific DMCs.

The 2015 Pacific SPI report found the coverage of social protection programs was improving but needed to be extended further; that spending on social insurance dominated other social protection categories and mostly benefited a relatively small number of formal sector workers; that social protection benefits remained limited for most poor people, and social assistance programs did not fully support the vulnerable due to inadequate coverage and small benefits; and that active LMPs were especially underdeveloped.[65]

This report comes to similar conclusions. It notes, however, small—but significant—changes, in particular the introduction of more universal benefits to vulnerable groups, such as all schoolchildren, the older population, and people with disabilities, thereby moving away from the tightly means-tested social

---

[65]   ADB. 2019. *The Social Protection Indicator for the Pacific: Assessing Progress.* Manila.

assistance programs that have been more common in the region. Moreover, there are significant references to social protection in the policy statements of many Pacific DMCs, signaling greater appreciation of the value of social protection against the vulnerabilities that Pacific island peoples and DMCs experience and perhaps heralding future change.

For example, in general men continue to benefit more than women from social protection, again reflecting the dominance of contributory social insurance programs and continued restrictions of women's economic opportunities. The rise in social assistance expenditures has benefited women more only when they are targeted. The progressive introduction of universal benefit schemes is generally benefiting men and women more equally.

The 2015 report also found, as a regional average, that only 31.2% of intended beneficiaries received the benefits to which they were entitled, leaving nearly two-thirds of eligible persons without support. Social assistance programs had, on average, the widest coverage, at 20.0% of intended beneficiaries; social insurance had narrower coverage of 8.7%; and active LMPs had the narrowest coverage of all, at 2.4%. In 2015, the average depth of programs in the Pacific region was equivalent to 50.6% of GDP per capita. This figure differed considerably between the three program categories. The average benefits of social insurance programs were much higher, at 140.6% of GDP per capita (an average value of $4,068.68). Social assistance programs had many more beneficiaries, but they received much smaller benefits, averaging 10.8% of GDP per capita ($627.91). Benefits were again lowest for active LMPs, at 11.2% of GDP per capita ($391.28). Again, the situation varied by country.

In 2018, this pattern only slightly changes. The regional average coverage is slightly higher, with just less than one-third (32.0%) of intended beneficiaries receiving the benefits to which they are entitled. Social assistance programs still have the widest coverage (19.1% of intended beneficiaries) but the smallest benefits (14.2% of GDP per capita). The coverage of social insurance programs remains low at 14.6%, but this marks an increase of almost two-thirds over the figure for 2015. Coverage for active LMPs still remains very low, at 4.3%, but this, too, represents some improvement over the situation in 2015.

The situation regarding the equitability of social protection expenditures between the poor and nonpoor has changed even less. Throughout the region, the poor benefit far less from social protection expenditures than the nonpoor, showing the continued dominance of contributory social insurance programs. The poor, however, fare best in DMCs with the least-developed social protection systems or where social insurance is not well developed—i.e., Vanuatu, Solomon Islands, Nauru, and Kiribati—which suggests that these DMCs may be able to transition to more equitable systems.

The 2015 report recommended that child assistance be expanded, that social protection be made more gender-sensitive, and that social protection policy frameworks be strengthened. These recommendations are repeated here. This report further recommends that governments consider the rights of all people to fully participate in their societies, particularly people with disabilities, children disadvantaged by factors such as remote locations or poor living conditions, and older people. In almost all Pacific DMCs, social assistance and active LMPs are affected by inadequate data management systems, limiting the potential of administrative records to assist with program management and policy development. It is therefore recommended that attention be given to upgrading administrative information systems pertaining to social protection, as has been done for education and health records in many Pacific DMCs.

IV. Social Protection for People with Disabilities

Introduction

For the first time, the SPI study gathers data on people with disabilities who benefit from social protection policies and programs. It calculates the proportion of social protection expenditure that is reaching people with disabilities in the region as well as the number of beneficiaries. This initiative follows commitments made by ADB in 2018 at the Global Disability Summit.[66] This also reflects commitments made to address poverty and to reduce inequalities in Strategy 2030.[67]

Global and regional development priorities in the Pacific region are focused on achieving the Sustainable Development Goals (SDGs) by 2030. The SDGs call on the world to "leave no one behind" and refer to people with disabilities in various targets.[68] They require the disaggregation of key indicators for people with disabilities, so that existing inequities can be revealed and that actions can address them. This SPI disaggregation for people with disabilities thus hopes to contribute to this work.

People with disabilities in the Asia and Pacific region are among the poorest, often lacking access to education, social protection, health and care services, employment, and livelihood opportunities; facing barriers in the built environment, transport, and communications; and in accessing information and assistive technology.[69] Indeed, poverty and disability are widely recognized as being interrelated. People who are poor are more likely to become disabled because of the conditions in which they live, and disabilities are likely to make people poorer because of discrimination and inequality of access to education and employment.[70]

---

[66] On 24 July 2018, the Department for International Development of the United Kingdom, along with the International Disability Alliance and Government of Kenya, hosted the first Global Disability Summit in London. Along with other multilateral development banks and international institutions, ADB made nine commitments to support disability inclusion across areas of investment and research, including analysis of data on social protection coverage for persons with disabilities in the Asia and Pacific region from the SPI database.

[67] ADB. 2018. *Strategy 2030: Achieving a Prosperous, Inclusive, Resilient, and Sustainable Asia and the Pacific.* Manila.

[68] The SDGs are universal and apply to all people equally. People with disabilities are specifically mentioned 11 times in the 2030 Agenda for Sustainable Development and especially in relation to SDGs 4 on education; 8 on employment; 10 on economic, social, and political inclusion; 11 on accessible cities, water, and transport; as well as 17 on data and monitoring. See United Nations. n.d. Disability-Inclusive Sustainable Development Goals. https://www.un.org/disabilities/documents/sdgs/disability_inclusive_sdgs.pdf.

[69] ADB. 2022. *Strengthening Disability-Inclusive Development: 2021–2025 Road Map.* Manila.

[70] GSDRC. Poverty and Disability. https://gsdrc.org/topic-guides/disability-inclusion/the-situation-of-people-with-disabilities/poverty-and-disability/; and UNESCAP. 2018. *Building Disability-Inclusive Societies in Asia and the Pacific: Assessing Progress of the Incheon Strategy.* Bangkok.

In 22 Pacific countries and territories, more than 1.5 million people live with some form of disability, and half of all persons with disabilities are older than age 60 years, as disabilities increase with age.[71] In some such as Tonga and the Cook Islands, the population is rapidly aging, which is contributing to the increased prevalence of disability. The prevalence of disabilities resulting from noncommunicable diseases, such as diabetes-related amputations and blindness, is also rising globally. This is particularly an issue in the Pacific region, as some DMCs such as Fiji, Samoa, and Tonga, have diabetes rates much higher than the 10% global prevalence.[72] Due to its aging population and high prevalence of some diseases, the population of the Pacific region is likely, in the next few decades, to have a rising percentage of people with disabilities.

Governments in the Pacific are generally unprepared for this demographic transition. This will result in wider social and economic consequences, but the levels of social protection coverage in the region remain low. In Asia and the Pacific, only 28%–30% of persons with disabilities are currently benefiting from social protection measures, such as government-funded health care, and only 9.4% of people with severe disabilities are covered by disability benefits.[73] Box 15 discusses mechanisms to strengthen the Convention on the Rights of Persons with Disabilities (CRPD) implementation in the Pacific.

This chapter provides a brief overview of disability-inclusive social protection in the Pacific before presenting the challenges and results of the SPI for people with disabilities. Case studies of innovations in social protection for people with disabilities in the Pacific region are provided throughout the chapter.

Disability-Inclusive Social Protection in the Pacific

The CRPD recognizes, in Article 28, the right of people with disabilities to an adequate standard of living and to social protection. This includes access to appropriate and affordable services, devices, and other assistance for disability-related needs and expenses, as well as access to programs focused on social protection, poverty reduction, public housing, and retirement programs.[74] The 2012 Incheon Strategy accelerates the implementation of the CRPD; Goal 4 highlights the necessity of ensuring that people with disabilities have access to social protection on an equal basis with others, including having access to affordable disability services to enable independent living.[75]

---

71   M. Sharp. 2020. Background on the Pacific Group on Disability Statistics. Presentation. 16 July. https://www.washingtongroup-disability.com/fileadmin/uploads/wg/Documents/20-8b.pdf; and UNESCAP. 2018. *Building Disability-Inclusive Societies in Asia and the Pacific: Assessing Progress of the Incheon Strategy.* Bangkok.

72   UNDP. 2014. *The State of Human Development in the Pacific: A Report on Vulnerability and Exclusion in a Time of Rapid Change.* Suva. pp. 86–90.

73   ILO. 2021. *ILO World Social Protection Report 2020–22: Social Protection at the Crossroads—In Pursuit of a Better Future.* Geneva; and OHCHR. 2020. *Policy Guidelines for Inclusive Sustainable Development Goals: No Poverty.* Geneva.

74   United Nations. 2007. *Convention on the Rights of Persons with Disabilities.* New York.

75   UNESCAP. 2017. *Incheon Strategy to "Make the Right Real" for Persons with Disabilities in Asia and the Pacific.* Bangkok.

Box 15: Mechanisms to Strengthen Implementation of the Convention on the Rights of Persons with Disabilities

The **Cook Islands** ratified the Convention on the Rights of Persons with Disabilities (CRPD) in 2009 and developed the Disability Inclusive Development Policy, 2020–2025, which builds on previous versions of national disability policies and is aligned with the Pacific Framework for the Rights of Persons with Disabilities, 2016–2025. The Cook Islands National Disability Council—an organization of people with disabilities—represents and advocates for people with disabilities in the country.

Fiji ratified the CRPD in 2017, and the Rights of Persons with Disabilities Act, adopted in 2018, aligned national legislation with the CRPD. The country utilized the Washington Group questions in its national census that same year, resulting in the number of people with disabilities rising from 3.0% of the population in 2015 to 12.8% of the population in 2018. The Disability Unit was established in the Ministry of Women, Children and Poverty Alleviation in 2018; the Disability Allowance Scheme and Housing Assistance Program for people with disabilities, as well as sports grants for people with disabilities, were all introduced in that same year. The Economic Empowerment of Persons with Disabilities Program was also introduced in 2018 as part of wider labor market reforms beginning in 2010.

Kiribati ratified the CRPD in 2013 and used Washington Group questions in the national census in 2015 for the first time. The National Disability Policy and Action Plan, 2018–2021 was launched in 2018 and includes plans to develop the National Disability Inclusion Act by 2021. The National Building Code was amended in 2017 to require all new buildings to be disability accessible, and the Disability Inclusive Policy was introduced in 2016 to accompany an amendment to the Employment Code to provide protection to people with disabilities in employment. An employment quota for people with disabilities was introduced in 2018 in a further amendment. The Disability Support Allowance was introduced in 2019.

Papua New Guinea ratified the CRPD in 2013 and adopted the National Policy on Disability, 2015–2025. The policy states that "[disability is an evolving concept…[it] results from the interaction between persons with impairments and attitudinal and environment barriers that hinder full and effective participation in society on an equal basis with others." A rights-based definition of disability, this is in line with the CRPD definition of disability.

Sources: ADB. 2022. *Cook Islands: Social Protection Indicator*. Manila; ADB. 2022. *Fiji: Social Protection Indicator*. Manila; ADB. 2022. *Kiribati: Social Protection Indicator*; and ADB. 2022. *Papua New Guinea: Social Protection Indicator*.

In 2016, members of the Pacific Islands Forum adopted the Pacific Framework for the Rights of Persons with Disabilities, 2016–2025.[76] The framework promotes and ensures the rights of persons with disabilities while providing regional strengthening of coordination and collaboration in support of associated national initiatives. Goal 1 aims to ensure inclusive employment and to promote livelihood opportunities for people with disabilities. Goal 2 emphasizes mainstreaming, which includes ensuring that people with disabilities have equal access to a range of rights, including social protection. Outcome 1 of Goal 2 also emphasizes the importance of ensuring that national policies, programs, and budgets include and benefit persons with disabilities and that their monitoring and reporting are disability inclusive.

---

[76] All DMCs are also members of the Pacific Islands Forum, an intergovernment body established in 1971 that fosters cooperation between governments and collaboration with international agencies. See Pacific Islands Forum. https://www.forumsec.org/who-we-arepacific-islands-forum/.

Goal 5 is focused on improving disability statistics and data.[77] Together with the Pacific Group on Disability Statistics, this represents increasing attention to—and a strong foundation for—disability-inclusive social protection in the Pacific (Figure 20).

Figure 20: International and Regional Framework on Disability and Social Protection

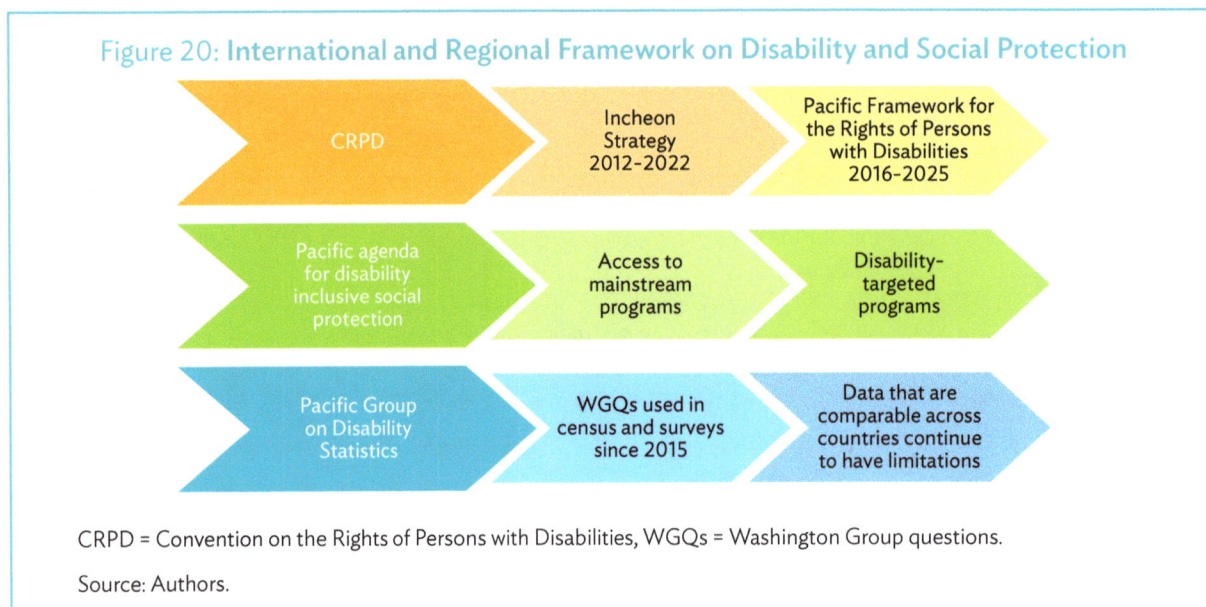

CRPD = Convention on the Rights of Persons with Disabilities, WGQs = Washington Group questions.

Source: Authors.

Globally, disability-inclusive social protection means ensuring access to (i) general social protection programs that aim to reduce poverty or to provide adequate income in old age, as well as (ii) disability-targeted programs that address the extra costs associated with disability in which being recognized as having a disability is the main criterion for access to a program. Disability-targeted programs improve consumption for people with disabilities and can include both contributory and noncontributory cash benefits or pensions; social services; and other support, such as personal assistance, assistive devices and technology, and caregiver allowances.[78]

The added costs of disability can cause significant inequities, so social protection programs that take into account these costs are better able to lift people with disabilities out of poverty.[79] In 2018, the United Nations Department of Economic and Social Affairs compiled estimates of the additional costs of disability, demonstrating that these extra costs as a percentage of average income can range from 8% to 43%. In Australia, for example, the extra costs of a "moderate" disability are 30% of an average income; for a "severe" disability, these are 40% of an average income.[80] Many social protection programs aimed at guaranteeing a minimum income do not take into account the additional costs of disability when calculating eligibility, however.

Common barriers to accessing social protection programs for people with disabilities can include constrained physical access to offices and service providers where benefits are administered; lack of information about programs and application requirements; and

---

[77]   Pacific Islands Forum. 2018. *Pacific Framework for the Rights of Persons with Disabilities, 2016–2025*. Suva.
[78]   UNESCAP. 2021. *How to Design Disability-Inclusive Social Protection*. Bangkok.
[79]   OHCHR. 2020. *Policy Guidelines for Inclusive Sustainable Development Goals: No Poverty*. Geneva.
[80]   UNDESA. 2019. *Disability and Development Report*. New York. pp. 37–38.

stigma and discrimination by social protection personnel. Many people with disabilities—especially those who were born with disabilities—have little or no education, and their literacy levels can be low compared with those of people without disabilities. They may find it difficult, therefore, to navigate complex application procedures or compliance conditions.[81] People with disabilities often have lower access to financial and banking services, mobile phones, and other important instruments of distributing social assistance as well.[82] Providing information in accessible formats; ensuring that eligibility criteria do not exclude people with disabilities; and providing physically accessible administration offices for benefits, inclusive data management systems, and accessible payment methods can all contribute to facilitating the access of people with disabilities to social protection programs.

The goals of disability-targeted programs depend on the political and social context in a country. In many, support for people with disabilities is closely associated with compensation for being unable to work. In this context, disability assessments are linked to the assessment of the capacity to work. In others, support for enabling daily functioning and maximizing the ability to live independently drive the design of disability-targeted programs. In Fiji, for example, eligibility is based on an assessment of support needs (Box 16). In most countries with disability-targeted programs, a medical assessment is part of the process for conferring disability status, eligibility for disability-targeted programs, and extra needs in general social protection programs.

Box 16: Disability Assessment in Fiji

In 2018, Fiji's Rights of Persons with Disabilities Act No. 4 defined disabilities as any condition that involves any loss or abnormality of the psychological, physiological, or anatomical structure or function of the body, including (i) sensory impairments, such as those affecting sight or hearing; (ii) impairments with fluctuating or recurring effects such as rheumatoid arthritis, myalgic encephalomyelitis/chronic fatigue syndrome, fibromyalgia, depression, and epilepsy; (iii) progressive impairment, such as motor neuron disease, muscular dystrophy, and forms of dementia and lupus; (iv) developmental impairment, such as autistic spectrum disorders, dyslexia, and dyspraxia; (v) learning difficulties; or (vi) mental health conditions and mental illnesses, such as depression, schizophrenia, eating disorders, bipolar affective disorders, obsessive compulsive disorders, as well as personality disorders.

Registration of people with disabilities is managed by the National Council for Persons with Disabilities, through the Ministry of Women, Children and Poverty Alleviation. The disability assessment is not medically driven but instead is focused on support needs of the person. A medical certificate may be required only if the social welfare officer carrying out the assessment is not in a position to make a decision.

New assistance programs for people with disabilities were introduced in 2018, the largest and most comprehensive being the Disability Allowance Scheme, a cash benefit provided to all registered people with disabilities and intended to cover the extra living costs related to disabilities. The number of people registered for disability-targeted social protection programs more than quadrupled in 2018 to 113,595 people compared with 26,070 people in 2015.

Source: ADB. 2022. *Fiji: Social Protection Indicator*. Manila.

[81] UNESCAP. 2018. *Building Disability-Inclusive Societies in Asia and the Pacific: Assessing Progress of the Incheon Strategy.* Bangkok.

[82] V. Barca, M. Hebber, and A. Cote. 2021. *SPACE Inclusive Information Systems for Social Protection: Intentionally Integrating Gender and Disability.* Washington, DC: Georgetown Institute for Women, Peace and Security.

In the Cook Islands, one disability-targeted social protection program is the Infirm Benefit. In 2018, it provides NZ$200 per month to 192 people with disabilities as a form of income support. However, this represents merely 6.6% of the population of 2,914 people with disabilities who are identified by the Cook Islands Statistics Office data or only 23.0% of 840 people with disabilities registered in the Cook Islands Disability Database. As many people with disabilities are clearly not receiving this form of social assistance, the Cook Islands National Disability Council admits that there may be gaps in awareness about the Infirm Benefit among people with disabilities.

In 2020, the amount doubled to NZ$400 per month. People with disabilities welcome the increase but also noted that "NZ$400 per month is enough to eat but not to do much else," which confirms that although it provides some level of social security, it fails to consider disability-related costs.[83]

In Nauru, a disability assessment is conducted by a medical team (i.e., a doctor and nurse) using questions focused on functioning.[84] Two negative responses are considered a "mild disability," three a "moderate disability," and four a "severe disability." Only people with a "severe disability," however, are eligible for the disability allowance.[85]

In Niue, the Welfare Committee decides on the eligibility of applicants for the Welfare Disability Benefit, a disability-targeted social assistance allowance, and payment ceases if the recipient finds employment.[86] As noted previously, citizens of the Cook Islands and Niue are also citizens of New Zealand and are eligible to receive similar benefits in New Zealand, where they go to access better medical treatment, care, and accessibility opportunities. This may affect the numbers of people registering for benefits in these DMCs.

Social services and independent living services are also fundamental to maximizing the inclusion of people with disabilities in mainstream education, employment, and social participation. Figure 21 illustrates how access to general cash benefits as well as disability-targeted benefits and social services—including assistive devices and rehabilitation services—together provide the building blocks for social protection for people with disabilities.

Several Pacific DMCs provide such services through nongovernment organizations (NGOs) and with funding from donors or development partners (Box 17). These services are often not funded by the national budget—with Samoa and Tonga being exceptions—so the expenditure on these services is not included in the SPI calculations. These services are nevertheless an important pillar of overall social protection systems and are often regulated and coordinated by government agencies. Regional organizations of people with disabilities, such as the Pacific

---

[83]   ADB. 2022. *Cook Islands: Social Protection Indicator*. Manila.
[84]   Are you able to dress yourself? Are you able to clean yourself after ablution? Are you able to feed yourself? Are you able to work?
[85]   ADB. 2022. *Nauru: Social Protection Indicator*. Manila.
[86]   ADB. 2022. *Niue: Social Protection Indicator*. Manila.

Figure 21: Building Blocks of Social Protection for People with Disabilities

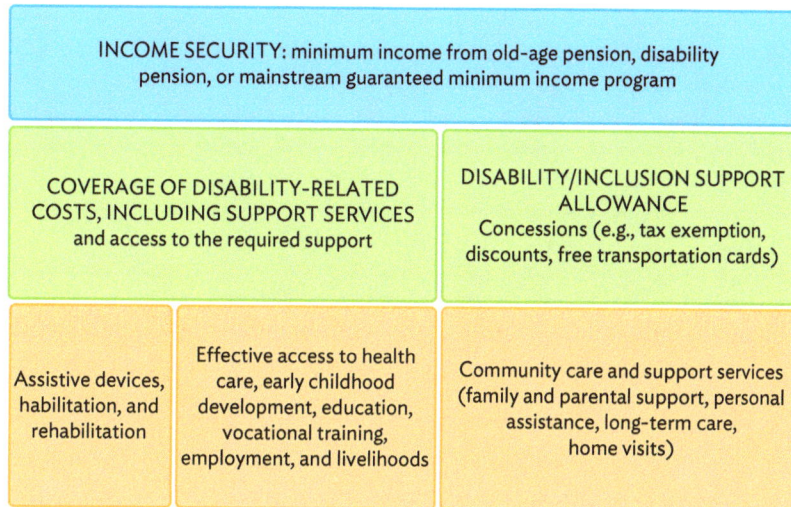

INCOME SECURITY: minimum income from old-age pension, disability pension, or mainstream guaranteed minimum income program

COVERAGE OF DISABILITY-RELATED COSTS, INCLUDING SUPPORT SERVICES and access to the required support

DISABILITY/INCLUSION SUPPORT ALLOWANCE
Concessions (e.g., tax exemption, discounts, free transportation cards)

Assistive devices, habilitation, and rehabilitation

Effective access to health care, early childhood development, education, vocational training, employment, and livelihoods

Community care and support services (family and parental support, personal assistance, long-term care, home visits)

Source: C. Knox-Vydmanov, A. Côte, F. Juergens, and D. Hiscock. 2021. Social Protection and Older Persons with Disabilities. Draft.

Disability Forum[87] and its national members, such as the Vanuatu Society for People with Disability and Fiji Disabled People's Federation, also contribute to advocacy and raising awareness of disability-inclusive social protection in the region.

Box 17: Examples of Services for People with Disabilities Supported by Nongovernment Partners

Federated States of Micronesia. The Federated States of Micronesia's Department of Education and Department of Health and Social Affairs receive funding from the Government of the United States to support the provision of inclusive education, health, and related social services to children and youth with disabilities up to age 21 years. Intellectual disability services and behavioral health services for children, especially in early childhood, are also supported. There are no services for adults with disabilities. Other services from a range of agencies including organizations of people with disabilities are coordinated, but not funded, through a government interagency collaboration agreement.

Samoa. The government funds six nongovernment organizations (NGOs) and organizations of people with disabilities to provide a range of services under special needs programs. Support for these programs is provided by the Government of Australia, through the Ministry of Education and Sports. The beneficiaries of the programs are children and young people with disabilities.

Tonga. Health assistance for vulnerable older people and special assistance to children with disabilities are both services implemented by an NGO, Ma'a Fafine mo e Famili, and funded by the Social Protection and Disability Division of the Ministry of Internal Affairs. The expenditure on these services in 2018 is included in the Social Protection Indicator (SPI) calculation.

continued on next page

---

87   Pacific Disability Forum. https://pacificdisability.org/.

Box 17: *continued*

Cook Islands. Support services for people with disabilities are provided by NGOs including the Creative Centre Rarotonga, which provides education programs for adults with disabilities; Te Vaerua, which provides physiotherapy services; Te Kainga Mental Health and Wellbeing Centre, which provides mental health support; and Are Pa Metua, which provides social programs for older people, many of whom have disabilities. People with disabilities rely on and value these services; one person with disabilities said, "We would be hidden without them," during a focus group discussion. Expenditure by the government on these services is not recorded in the 2018 SPI report.

Sources: ADB. 2022. *Cook Islands: Social Protection Indicator.* Manila; ADB. 2022. *Federated States of Micronesia: Social Protection Indicator.* Manila; ADB. 2022. *Samoa: Social Protection Indicator.* Manila; and ADB. 2022. *Tonga: Social Protection Indicator.* Manila.

Measuring Social Protection Coverage for People with Disabilities

1.   Definition of Disability

All but one DMC in the Pacific region—Niue—has either signed or ratified the CRPD.[88] The CRPD definition of persons with disabilities are those "who have long-term physical, mental, intellectual or sensory impairments which in interaction with various barriers may hinder their full and effective participation in society on an equal basis with others"; however, national definitions in the Pacific are generally not aligned with this.[89]

Assessment of people with disabilities in the region generally continues to be medically focused—rather than enveloping a holistic assessment of social, medical, and personal characteristics and barriers in the environment that create the disability—despite CRPD ratification. In the FSM, for example, children become eligible for special education and other services automatically if they fit under 1 of 13 disability categories: autism, blindness, deafness, emotional disturbance, intellectual disability, multiple disabilities, orthopedic impairment, other health impairment, specific learning disabilities, speech impairment, language impairment, traumatic brain injury, and/or visual impairment.[90] This is an example of a medically focused assessment that considers a diagnosis rather than the individual concerned. A disability has varying degrees, so a disability assessment should be highly individualized and not simply categorize an individual according to a single, one-size-fits-all diagnosis. Indeed, in some countries, even if the definition of disability is aligned with the CRPD in national legislation and policy, at assessment—that is, the moment when disability is defined for an individual—an overly medical approach

---

[88]   Solomon Islands and Tonga have both signed but not yet ratified the CRPD.
[89]   United Nations. 2007. *Convention on the Rights of Persons with Disabilities.* New York. p. 4.
[90]   ADB. 2022. *Federated States of Micronesia: Social Protection Indicator.* Manila.

continues to be practiced. Thus, overall, there is a need to continue to strengthen the legal framework and implementation of the CRPD in many DMCs.[91]

2.   Identification of People with Disabilities

Defining the population of people with disabilities—and therefore defining the reference population for social protection programs targeting people with disabilities—is challenging in all Pacific DMCs. Stigma, discrimination, complex assessment procedures, or other barriers may mean that people are not motivated to register with governments as disabled. Thus, disability prevalence estimates based on registered people with disabilities can significantly undercount the number of people with disabilities in a population.

Since the CRPD was introduced in 2006, several initiatives have worked to address these challenges, resulting in the development of the World Health Organization (WHO) Disability Assessment Schedule 2.0 and Washington Group questions (WGQs).[92] In 2013, the Washington Group on Disability Statistics identified the Pacific region as needing support in strengthening its disability statistics. In 2016, the Pacific Group on Disability Statistics was convened by several governments in the region, Washington Group on Disability Statistics, and the Pacific Community[93] and supported by the Department of Foreign Affairs and Trade (DFAT), Government of Australia. This platform was formally established in 2020 and continues to build the region's capacity to collect disability statistics.[94] As a result of these efforts, the governments of the Pacific region have used the WGQs in censuses and surveys conducted since 2015, many of which were used in the SPI reports.

Identifying people with disabilities, nevertheless, remains challenging. Data that are comparable across DMCs continue to be limited, largely because methods vary. Moreover, disability is always understood in relation to perceptions of normal functioning and is therefore influenced by contextual factors such as age, sex, and even income group.[95] Older people may not think of themselves as having a disability although they experience considerable difficulties in functioning because they perceive these challenges as normal for their ages. Similarly, parents or caregivers who answer questions about their children may not accurately report their children's difficulties in functioning, because of stigma, fear of admitting difficulties, or differing perceptions

---

[91]   Pacific Disability Forum. 2018. *Pacific Disability Forum SDG-CRPD Monitoring Report 2018—From Recognition to Realisation of Rights: Furthering Effective Partnership for an Inclusive Pacific 2030.* Suva. p. 4.

[92]   The Washington Group Questions Short Set asks if a person has "no difficulty," "some difficulty," "a lot of difficulty," or "cannot do at all" in six domains of functioning: vision, hearing, mobility, cognition (i.e., remembering and concentrating), self-care, and communicating (i.e., understanding and being understood). Washington Group on Disability Statistics. 2020. *The Washington Group Short Set on Functioning (WG-SS).* https://www.washingtongroup-disability.com/fileadmin/uploads/wg/Documents/ Questions/Washington_Group_Questionnaire__1_-_WG_Short_Set_on_Functioning.pdf. See also WHO. 2012. *Measuring Health and Disability: Manual for WHO Disability Assessment Schedule (WHODAS 2.0).* Geneva.

[93]   The Pacific Community is a regional organization with 27 government members that provides technical and scientific support to the governments of the region to meet their development goals. See SPC. https://www.spc.int/about-us/history.

[94]   M. Sharp. 2020. Background on the Pacific Group on Disability Statistics. Presentation. 16 July. https://www.washingtongroup-disability.com/fileadmin/uploads/wg/Documents/20-8b.pdf.

[95]   WHO and World Bank. 2011. *World Report on Disability.* Geneva.

of what is considered normal functioning at different stages of development.
The way that questions are asked (i.e., face-to-face or by questionnaires) and the kind
of questions (i.e., focused on impairments, disability, or difficulties in functioning)
can also influence the resulting disability prevalence rates.

3.   Disability Prevalence Rate

The 2011 World Report on Disability used two global studies published in 2004—the
World Health Survey and Global Burden of Disease—to estimate the often-quoted
prevalence rate of 10%–15% of the world's adult population living with some disability
(footnote 95). These studies used different methods for determining disability,
and WHO and the International Labour Organization continue to use these estimates
as the denominator when calculating the coverage of people with disabilities by social
protection programs. WHO uses the rate of 2.7% for the Pacific, which represents the
proportion of the population with severe disabilities, equivalent to "cannot do at all"
according to the WGQs (footnote 95).

The WGQs are designed for use when asking questions to and about adults.
To address children, the United Nations Children's Fund (UNICEF) and the
Washington Group collaborated to develop the child functioning module.[96]
As mentioned previously, reliable data on children with disabilities are generally
challenging to collect, since parents and caregivers may hide their child's impairments
during surveys or may underestimate or overestimate their child's level of functioning
when compared with other children. In the Pacific region, the module has recently
been used in surveys in Kiribati, Samoa, and Tonga.[97]

The 2018 SPI study uses official government sources to identify the population of people
with disabilities who should be covered by social protection, including those from
national population and housing censuses, household income and expenditure surveys,
and labor force surveys, all conducted by national statistical offices. Table 17 sets out the
disability prevalence rates reported by the SPI country reports and sources of the data.

The prevalence rates are taken to apply to the whole population of a DMC, although
some surveys cited refer only to the adult population ages 18 years or older, and others
refer only to the population ages 15 years and older. The crude prevalence rates in
Table 17 cannot be applied therefore to children or to the population over age 60 years. All
surveys and censuses cited used the WGQs and included people with disabilities who said
they had "a lot of difficulty" and "cannot do at all" in at least one domain of functioning,
although DMCs with higher prevalence rates (e.g., the Cook Islands and Vanuatu) may
include a wider definition of "some difficulty" in at least one domain of functioning.

The Pacific Community has also coordinated the publication of disability prevalence
data in Pacific island countries based on official census and survey data. These data
differ, in some cases, from the prevalence rates presented in Table 17. Where there are
discrepancies, it is likely that slightly different population groups are being counted,

---

[96]   UNICEF. Child Functioning. https://data.unicef.org/topic/child-disability/data-collection-tools/module-
on-child-functioning/ (accessed 2 June 2022).
[97]   UNICEF. 2022. *Seen, Counted, Included: Using Data to Shed Light on the Well-Being of Children with
Disabilities.* New York.

Table 17: Disability Prevalence Rates Used to Calculate the Social Protection Indicator (%)

Country	Rate	Source
Cook Islands	18.3	ADB. 2022. *Cook Islands: Social Protection Indicator.* Manila.
Fiji	12.8	Fiji Bureau of Statistics. 2018. *Fiji 2017 Population and Housing Census.* Suva.
Kiribati	2.5	UNICEF Pacific, Kiribati National Statistics Office, and Pacific Community 2017. *Disability Monograph: From the 2015 Population and Housing Census.* Suva: UNICEF.
Marshall Islands	11.1	Government of the Republic of the Marshall Islands, Economic Policy, Planning, and Statistics Office. 2011. *Republic of the Marshall Islands 2011 Census Report.* Noumea: SPC.
FSM	11.1	ADB. 2022. *Federated States of Micronesia: Social Protection Indicator.* Manila.
Nauru	2.5	Nauru Bureau of Statistics. 2019. *2019 Population and Housing Census.* Yaren.
Niue	5.7	Statistics Niue. 2017. *2017 Population and Housing Census.* Alofi.
Palau	2.4	Government of Palau, Office of Planning and Statistics and UNDP. 2017. *Palau: Analysis of the 2014 Household Income and Expenditure Survey: Report on the Estimation of Basic Needs Poverty Lines and the Incidence and Characteristics of Hardship and Basic Needs Poverty in Palau.* Ngerulmud.
Papua New Guinea	1.5	National Statistical Office Papua New Guinea and ICF. 2019. *Papua New Guinea Demographic and Health Survey 2016–18.* Port Moresby.
Samoa	2.0	Samoa Bureau of Statistics. 2017. *Samoa Population and Housing Census 2016.* Apia.
Solomon Islands	2.3	Solomon Islands National Statistics Office. *Solomon Islands Population and Housing Census 2009.* Honiara.
Tonga	5.9	Tonga Statistics Department. 2017. *Tonga 2016 Census of Population and Housing: Volume 1—Basic Tables and Administrative Report.* Noumea: SPC.
Tuvalu	2.7	SPC 2017. *Tuvalu 2017 Mini Census Preliminary Report 1.* Noumea.
Vanuatu	2.4	SPC. 2013. *Vanuatu Demographic and Health Survey 2013.* Noumea.
Unweighted Average	5.9	

FSM = Federated States of Micronesia, ICF = Inner City Fund, SPC = Secretariat of the Pacific Community, UNDP = United Nations Development Programme, UNICEF = United Nations Children's Fund.

Source: Compiled by author.

for example, ages 15 years and older, working ages 15–59 years, or ages 15–50 years. In some cases, surveys or censuses conducted in different years may have used slightly different methodologies. In still others, there may be methodological differences with moderate disabilities (i.e., "some difficulty" in one domain according to the WGQs) included to give a higher disability prevalence as in the Cook Islands, or only "cannot do at all," giving a lower prevalence rate.

In some DMCs, there are multiple sources for disability-prevalence data. Tonga has data from a labor force survey conducted in 2018, giving a disability prevalence rate of 3.16% among working-age people.[98] The Pacific Community gives a rate of 4.60% from the census conducted in 2016.[99] The SPI country report uses the 2016 census data, for a 5.90% overall prevalence rate.

---

[98] Tonga Statistics Department. 2019. *2018 Labour Force Survey Report.* Nuku'alofa.
[99] Tonga Statistics Department. 2017. *Tonga 2016 Census of Population and Housing: Volume 1—Basic Tables and Administrative Report.* Noumea: SPC.

For the Cook Islands, disability data are collected through the census, which asks the WGQs. The 2016 census gave a rate of 4.36%.[100] According to the National Disability Database, there are 840 people with disabilities in 2019, which represents 5.00% of the population. The Statistics Office, however, provides a much larger prevalence rate—18.30%—based on "at least one physical disability" as reported in a 2018 survey. The SPI country report uses these Statistics Office data.

The Global Burden of Disease and World Health Survey both indicated much higher prevalence rates of disability among people ages 60 years and over since functional impairments increase with age. The disability rates among people ages 60 years and over in the WHO Western Pacific region are roughly the same as the global average, with 10% having a severe disability and 47% moderate and severe disabilities. Table 18 presents data from nine Pacific island countries for which disability data disaggregated by age are available, showing how rates vary with age.

Lower prevalence rates among children and higher prevalence rates among those ages 60 years and over, as reported in the SPI country reports, are consistent with the global and regional estimates from the Global Burden of Disease and World

Table 18: Disability Prevalence Rates among Different Age Groups and Rates from the Global Burden of Disease

(%)

Country	Ages 0–14 Years	Ages 15–59 Years	Ages 60 Years and Above	Whole Population
Cook Islands	2.7	18.7	41.0	18.3
Fiji	1.6	12.1	52.1	12.8
Kiribati	0.5	2.2	17.6	2.5
FSM	4.1	11.0	55.9	11.0
Nauru	1.8	2.1	15.0	2.5
Palau	0.7	0.6	15.4	2.5
Solomon Islands	1.8	2.2	6.5	2.3
Tonga	8.0	2.6	18.8	5.9
Tuvalu	0.4	1.8	15.1	2.7
Global Burden of Disease 2004 Western Pacific Region				
Severe disability	0.5	2.4	10.3	2.7
Moderate and severe disability	5.3	13.7	46.7	15.0

FSM = Federated States of Micronesia.

Note: The Western Pacific Region includes all Pacific island countries as well as the People's Republic of China, Japan, the Republic of Korea, Mongolia, and other countries in East Asia.

Source: WHO and World Bank. 2011. *World Report on Disability*. Geneva; and WHO Office of the Western Pacific. Where We Work. https://www.who.int/westernpacific/about/where-we-work.

---

[100] Cook Islands Statistics Office. 2010. *Cook Islands 2006 Census Report*. Noumea: SPC.

Health Survey. Significant variations among prevalence rates in different DMCs for the same age groups—for example, over 50% of older people have disabilities in Fiji and the FSM, compared with only 6% in Solomon Islands and 7% in Palau— can be accounted for by various methods and questions used in surveys, differing cultural norms and perceptions of disability in various contexts, as well as varying thresholds for defining disability (i.e., moderate or severe) in administrative data sets.[101] There may also be higher proportions of people in the older age ranges, such as ages 75 years and above in some DMCs, which translates into higher disability prevalence rates.[102]

In DMCs with stricter definitions of disability, the prevalence tends to increase from around 2% for adults to 15% for older people. In those with broader definitions of disability, the rates tend to go from 10%–12% for adults to 40%–50% for older people (Figure 22).

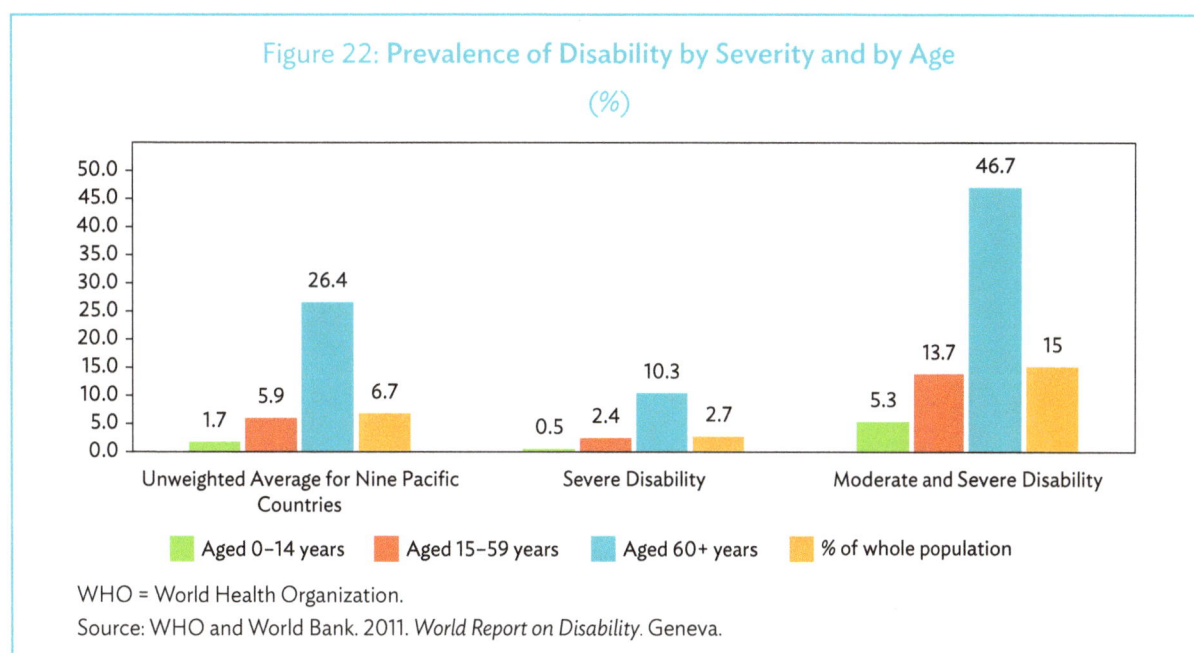

Figure 22: **Prevalence of Disability by Severity and by Age**

(%)

WHO = World Health Organization.
Source: WHO and World Bank. 2011. *World Report on Disability*. Geneva.

The use of WGQs in surveys and national censuses is a positive step forward in generating reliable, comparable data on disability prevalence. A useful next step is to include WGQs in social, health, and education registries and then follow up with disability assessments for the provision of benefits and services. These approaches can provide more accurate data to support planning of social protection programs. This is important as the needs of people with disabilities change throughout the life cycle and cut across government sectors such as education, health, social protection, housing, employment, transport, and civic participation.

---

[101] Government of the Cook Islands. 2020. *Cook Islands Disability Inclusive Development Policy: Rights/ Responsibilities/Action, 2020–2025*. Avarua. p. 17.
[102] WHO and World Bank. 2011. *World Report on Disability*. Geneva.

Early intervention and early childhood development can impact education and employment outcomes for people with disabilities.[103] In Tonga, however, only 14% of 3- to 4-year-olds with functional difficulties are in early childhood education programs, compared with 37% of children without functional difficulties.[104] In Kiribati, 21% of lower-secondary school-aged children with functional difficulties are not attending school, compared with 8% of children without functional difficulties. Moreover, adolescents with disabilities, especially with the most severe disabilities, are significantly more likely than their peers without disabilities to not be attending school (footnote 104). Globally, the poverty rate for adults with disabilities ages 19–40 years is greater than people without disabilities of the same ages,[105] illustrating the importance of education in childhood and consequent employment in adulthood and their relationship to poverty.

It is also important for governments to understand the prevalence of disability in the aging population so that they can forecast the need for different types of social services—especially care services—and plan to meet the demand as it emerges. Samoa claims that only 288 people over age 60 years have disabilities; however, this represents only 1.8% of the population ages 60 years and over. A study in Niue conducted by the Economic Research Institute examined how the government could create the fiscal space to improve the situation of people with disabilities by increasing the benefit amount or coverage, showing how a relatively small cost could make a substantial difference.[106] Accurate data on disability prevalence at different ages can help ensure more targeted and effective policy responses— including social protection—that promote equity and social inclusion.

2018 Social Protection Indicator Results

As discussed in Chapters I–III, social insurance in the region has limited coverage, as it only covers people employed in the formal sector. People with disabilities are underrepresented in formal employment and are therefore unlikely to benefit significantly from social insurance. In the Cook Islands, for example, only 6 people received disability benefits under the social insurance program in 2018 out of a population of 840 people registered with disabilities. This means that disability-targeted social assistance programs are especially important for ensuring that people with disabilities are accessing social protection measures (Boxes 18 and 19).

In 7 of the 14 Pacific DMCs, there are no social assistance programs targeted to people with disabilities. In Samoa, it is likely that a large proportion of the recipients of the Senior Citizen's Benefit Scheme, for people ages 65 years and older, are people

---

[103] WHO and UNICEF. 2012. *Early Childhood Development and Disability: A Discussion Paper.* Geneva: WHO; WHO. 2018. *Nurturing Care for Early Childhood Development: A Framework for Helping Children Survive and Thrive to Transform Health and Human Potential.* Geneva; and CBM. 2016. *Inclusion Counts: The Economic Case for Disability Inclusive Development.* Bensheim. p. 60.

[104] UNICEF. 2022. *Seen, Counted, Included: Using Data to Shed Light on the Well-Being of Children with Disabilities.* New York. p. 68.

[105] UNDESA. 2019. *Disability and Development Report.* New York. pp. 34–37.

[106] ADB. 2022. *Niue: Social Protection Indicator.* Manila.

Box 18: Disability-Targeted Allowances and Benefits

Fiji. The Disability Allowance Scheme of F$90 per month is intended to help people with disabilities meet the extra costs that their disabilities incur. It is not means-tested and is available to all people with disabilities, regardless of whether they are employed or receive other forms of support, except for the Social Pension Scheme for older persons. The number of beneficiaries of the Disability Allowance Scheme increased from 2,744 in 2018 to 7,003 people in 2019 to 8,662 people by August 2020, which represents 8% of people with disabilities as identified in the 2017 census using Washington Group questions. People with disabilities are also eligible for a credit of F$40 per month for travel by bus and up to F$2,000 for livelihood programs. In addition, free health services, including rehabilitation, prosthetics, or mobility devices, are available to people with disabilities. The Housing Assistance Scheme for people with disabilities provides help modifying housing to suit different disabilities as well.

Cook Islands. The Total and Permanent Disablement Benefit is a social insurance benefit that is paid as a lump sum if a person has made the necessary contributions to the Cook Islands National Superannuation Fund and becomes totally or permanently disabled due to injury or illness. Six people received this payment in 2018. The Infirm Allowance is part of the social protection floor for people with disabilities over age 16 years who obtain a medical certificate and are unable to support themselves due to a disability. The Special Assistance Fund is for assistive devices for people who have severe physical disabilities and are dependent on a caregiver. It is also for enabling accessibility at home for older people with impairments who live alone, with only a pension as income. The Caregiver Allowance is provided to people who are unemployed and are caring for an older person or a person with disability with high care needs.

Nauru. Nauru became one of the first countries in the region to introduce a disability allowance in 2008. The amount has increased five times, from A$50 per fortnight when first introduced to A$250 per fortnight in the 2020–2021 budget. The allowance was received by 159 people with disabilities in 2018, or 1.5% of the population. The disability allowance cannot be combined with other social welfare schemes or with income from employment.

Sources: ADB. 2022. *Cook Islands: Social Protection Indicator*. Manila; ADB. 2022. *Fiji: Social Protection Indicator*. Manila; and ADB. 2022. *Nauru: Social Protection Indicator*. Manila.

Box 19: Disability-Inclusive Employment and Technical and Vocational Education and Training in Solomon Islands

Two rural training centers in San Isidro and Bethesda provide life skills training to people with disabilities in agriculture, woodwork or carpentry, business management, cooking, and sewing. Bethesda's center, in particular, follows training with support to graduates with the most potential in the form of finance for materials and supplies to start their own businesses or to help them find jobs. Other graduates receive other types of support with economic engagement. This program is funded mainly by nongovernment organizations with some funding from the government.

The community-based rehabilitation network in Solomon Islands plays an important role in supporting access for people with disabilities to potential employers such as Kokonut Pacific Solomon Islands, a for-profit social enterprise producing and selling virgin coconut oil and products with a mission focused on the development and empowerment of remote villages. Cooperation with community-based rehabilitation has led to employment opportunities for persons with disabilities in the enterprise, and accessibility facilities have been added to the Kokonut Pacific Solomon Islands workshop.

continued on next page

Box 19: *continued*

Fourteen percent of beneficiaries of the Youth-at-Work Program implemented by the Secretariat of the Pacific Community and Youth Division of the Ministry of Women, Youth, Children and Family Affairs are young people with disabilities. The program addresses youth unemployment by aiding the placement of young people onto career pathways, with the objective of helping them access paid employment or start their own businesses. In 2018, 550 youths, including 77 youths with disabilities, benefited from the program with assistance to start small businesses, find job placements, and attend trainings. The United Nations Development Programme and Australia's Department of Foreign Affairs and Trade also support this program alongside the Government of Solomon Islands.

Sources: Pacific Disability Forum. 2018. *Pacific Disability Forum SDG-CRPD Monitoring Report 2018—From Recognition to Realisation of Rights: Furthering Effective Partnership for an Inclusive Pacific 2030.* Suva. p. 17; and ADB. 2022. *Solomon Islands: Social Protection Indicator.* Manila.

with disabilities. Without disaggregated data or a disability prevalence rate for those ages 65 years and over, however, it is difficult to estimate the proportion of beneficiaries who are people with disabilities. Similarly, in Vanuatu, no programs target older people, but the SPI for people with disabilities assumes that about 5% of people receiving government scholarships, the Housing Allowance, Child Allowance, or noncommunicable disease and mental health programs are people with disabilities. This can only be verified through further research or the introduction of filter questions in the registration of people for these schemes.

Table 19 summarizes the types of programs in each DMC targeted to people with disabilities and the assumptions that have been made about participation of people with disabilities in general social protection programs when calculating the SPI for persons with disabilities.

The SPI for persons with disabilities presented in Table 20 considers both expenditures of programs targeted only to people with disabilities as explained in Table 19 as well as subsets of budgets of general social protection programs based on estimates of the proportion of beneficiaries who are people with disabilities. This SPI is generally a small part of the overall SPI for all Pacific DMCs. This is to be expected, as the population of people with disabilities is a small proportion of the overall population. The consultants preparing the country reports used estimates based on disability prevalence or household surveys to calculate the proportion of people with disabilities benefiting from general social protection programs as summarized in column 5 of Table 19. This means that untested assumptions have been made in many cases about how many people with disabilities are accessing general social protection programs and services.

In Tuvalu, for example, the register of people with disabilities was cross-checked with recipients of general social protection programs, such as the Tuvalu Senior Citizens Scheme, thereby confirming that people with disabilities are not benefiting from those programs. The SPIs for disability expenditure, therefore, rely on assumptions that have varying degrees of validity. Nevertheless, the SPIs demonstrate the weight

Table 19: Programs Benefiting People with Disabilities, 2018

Country	Disability Allowance (social assistance)	Disability Benefits (social insurance)	Other	% of Expenditure
Cook Islands	Infirm Benefit	Disablement Benefit, Cook Islands National Superannuation Fund	None	3%–52% of expenditure on Old Age Pension, Destitute Benefit, 8 other social assistance programs, and 5 other social insurance programs
Fiji	Disability Allowance	None	Housing Assistance Program, Economic Empowerment for People with Disabilities, sports grants for people with disabilities	1% of expenditure on bus fare for students and 10% of expenditure on bus fare concessions for older persons and people with disabilities
Kiribati	Disability support allowance (introduced in 2019 and not included in SPI for 2018)	Provident Fund Disability Benefits	100% school fees for underprivileged children, and 100% school fees for children with special needs	35% of expenditure on Senior Citizen's Benefit
Marshall Islands	None	Disability benefits	90% special education program	2%–11% of expenditure on 2 cash-for-work and 2 social assistance programs
FSM	None	Disability benefit	55% special education program	5% of expenditure for 3 other social insurance programs including Retirement Benefit
Nauru	Disability Allowance	None	None	None
Niue	Welfare Disability Benefit	None	None	5.7% of expenditure on Niue Pension and Welfare Hardship Benefit
Palau	Severely Disabled Assistance Fund	None	100% special education program	58% aging program (i.e., home meals and center) 1%–10% of expenditure on other programs based on disability prevalence assumptions or program criteria (e.g., 10% of places in early care and education program earmarked for children with disabilities)
Papua New Guinea	None	None	None	1% of expenditure on 2 national social fund retirement programs
Samoa	None	None	80%–95% beneficiaries of 6 civil society organization services	None
Solomon Islands	None	None	100% disability training, 52% community-based rehabilitation, 14% youth at work (all based on actual data)	None

continued on next page

Table 19: *continued*

Country	Disability Allowance (social assistance)	Disability Benefits (social insurance)	Other	% of Expenditure
Tonga	None	None	None	3%–25% of expenditure on people of relevant age group based on prevalence in 2016 census applied to 5 social insurance, 5 social assistance, and 1 labor market program
Tuvalu	Disability assistance	None	None	Names of recipients of other programs were cross-checked with the list of people with disabilities provided by the Social Welfare Department, and none were benefiting from other programs
Vanuatu	None	None	None	3%–5% of expenditure on 4 social assistance programs
Total	6 (and 1 in 2019)	4	18	

FSM = Federated States of Micronesia, SPI = Social Protection Indicator.

Source: 2022 SPI country reports.

Table 20: Maximum and Minimum Disability Social Protection Indicator for People with Disabilities
(%)

Country	Overall SPI	Maximum Disability SPI	Maximum Disability SPI Divided by Total SPI	Minimum Disability SPI	Minimum Disability SPI Divided by Total SPI	Disability Prevalence Rate
Cook Islands	3.3	1.3	39.4	0.1	3.0	18.3
Fiji	3.3	0.1	3.0	0.1	3.0	12.8
Kiribati	11.1	0.7	6.3	0.4	3.6	2.5
Marshall Islands	10.3	1.0	9.7	0.9	8.7	11.1
FSM	5.0	1.1	22.0	0.3	6.0	11.1
Nauru	2.9	0.4	13.8	0.4	13.8	2.5
Niue	7.8	0.4	5.1	0.1	1.3	5.7
Palau	10.4	1.0	9.6	1.0	9.6	2.4
Papua New Guinea	0.9	0.0	0.0	0.0	0.0	1.5
Samoa	3.4	0.01	0.3	0.01	0.3	2.0
Solomon Islands	3.0	0.0	0.0	0.0	0.0	2.3
Tonga	1.5	0.2	13.3	0.03	2.0	5.9
Tuvalu	10.7	0.1	0.9	0.1	0.9	2.7
Vanuatu	3.4	0.1	3.0	0.1	3.0	2.4
Unweighted Average	5.5	0.5	9.1	0.3	4.0	5.9

SPI = Social Protection Indicator., FSM = Federated States of Micronesia

Source: 2022 SPI country reports.

of disability status within the overall social protection system, since they show the social protection expenditure for disability as a percentage of the overall social protection expenditure.

On average, across the Pacific DMCs, the SPI for persons with disabilities is 0.5% of GDP per capita, out of the overall SPI of 5.5% of GDP per capita. Only about 9.0% of social protection expenditures go to people with disabilities; this assumes that people with disabilities are benefiting from general social protection programs as well as disability-targeted programs. If calculated only with programs that are targeted to people with disabilities (i.e., in which 100% of beneficiaries are people with disabilities), the SPI for persons with disabilities is 0.3% of GDP per capita or 4.0% of the overall SPI. Given the lack of disaggregated data on people with disabilities benefiting from general social assistance or social insurance programs, it is difficult to know the actual SPI for persons with disabilities, however.

The average disability prevalence rate for the Pacific DMCs is 5.9%, and the SPI for programs targeted to people with disabilities is 4.0% of the overall SPI. This indicates that people with disabilities are largely not receiving a proportional amount of social protection expenditure.

Table 20 presents the data on the proportion of the overall SPI that is reaching people with disabilities, using the maximum and minimum estimates of social protection. In the minimum SPI for disability, only disability-targeted programs are included. In the maximum SPI for disability, the attribution of people with disabilities benefiting from general social protection programs can only be considered a rough estimate. The data in Tables 19 and 20 demonstrate the need for disaggregation of people with disabilities among the beneficiaries of general social protection expenditures and for clarity on the overlaps among different programs if a robust understanding of the level of social protection expenditure for people with disabilities is to be gained.

It should be noted that in calculating the SPI for persons with disabilities, expenditure on disability services—including, for example, day-care services, community-based rehabilitation services, and housing assistance—is included as social assistance for some DMCs. Reasons may include that there are no such services in some DMCs; such services exist but expenditures cannot be distinctly identified (e.g., the FSM and the Cook Islands, where social services for people with disabilities are provided by CSOs or funded directly by development partners and are not captured in the SPI); or such services belong to other sectors (e.g., health sector programs include rehabilitation services and provision of orthopedic or assistive devices that are included as social assistance or social insurance expenditure). PNG, Tonga, and Vanuatu do not have any disability-targeted programs, but this does not mean that people with disabilities do not benefit from other social protection programs; programs targeted to people with disabilities and funded from the state budget are not included in the minimum SPI calculation.

Based on Table 20, PNG, Samoa, and Solomon Islands appear to have little or no expenditures on people with disabilities. Samoa is, however, funding six CSO programs delivering services to people with disabilities. These expenditures are included in the SPI calculation, but it is such a small percentage of the overall social protection expenditure that its SPI for people with disabilities is still only 0.01% of GDP per capita.

In PNG, disability benefits are associated with the national insurance scheme, but in the absence of data on the number of people with disabilities who are benefiting, these are not included in the SPI calculation. Only 1% of a social assistance program for older people is included in the SPI for people with disabilities, and this is given an SPI of 0%, again as the expenditure is insignificant. In Solomon Islands, the government is funding a community-based inclusive development program benefiting 25% of the population of people with disabilities, but only a small amount is counted in the SPI, as it is funded from nongovernment sources.

To examine trends over time in social protection expenditures targeted to people with disabilities, ADB also examines these expenditures as a share of GDP. These have increased since 2009 in most Pacific DMCs, albeit from a low base (Table 21).

The data presented in Table 21 have some limitations, as the definition of "disability expenditures" depends on how the ADB consultants defined programs in previous years. For 2018, more attention is given to this issue, and the data are of better quality. Overall, DMCs can be grouped into four categories relating to how expenditure on

Table 21: Share of Disability-Targeted Social Protection Expenditures to Gross Domestic Product, 2009–2018

(% of GDP per capita)

	2009	2012	2015	2018
Cook Islands	...	0.120	0.090	0.110
Fiji	0.050	...	...	0.150
FSM	...	0.450	0.480	0.430
Kiribati	...	0.720	0.160	0.390
Nauru	0.100	0.120	0.740	0.520
Palau	0.300	0.010	0.360	0.460
Papua New Guinea	...	...	...	...
Marshall Islands	0.200	0.450	0.450	1.040
Samoa	...	0.010	0.070	0.010
Solomon Islands	0.004	...	...	0.000
Tonga	...	0.010	0.040	0.040
Tuvalu	...	...	...	0.200
Vanuatu	0.040	...	...	...
Unweighted Average	0.100	0.200	0.300	0.300

... = no data or program, GDP = gross domestic product, FSM = Federated States of Micronesia.

Source: 2022 Social Protection Indicator country reports.

disability in social protection has changed as a percentage of GDP, depending on whether the level of expenditure has moved from lower to higher, from higher to lower, remained low, or remained high (Figure 23).

Figure 23: **Trends in Expenditure on Disability-Focused Social Protection, 2009–2018**

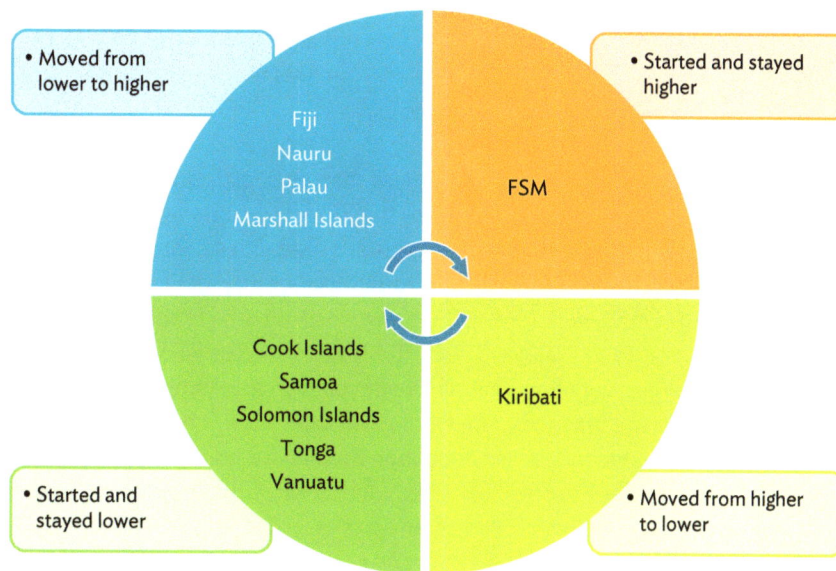

- Moved from lower to higher

- Started and stayed higher

Fiji
Nauru
Palau
Marshall Islands

FSM

Cook Islands
Samoa
Solomon Islands
Tonga
Vanuatu

Kiribati

- Started and stayed lower

- Moved from higher to lower

FSM = Federated States of Micronesia.
Source: 2022 Social Protection Indicator country reports.

The tendency over time is toward increased attention to disability in social protection, and it is notable that nonfinancial data confirm this trend. Domestic expenditure on disability inclusion still is generally less than 0.1% of GDP for many DMCs in 2018, however.[107] Table 19 illustrates the emergence of new disability allowances and other disability-targeted programs that have increased social protection expenditure directed toward people with disabilities. This does not mean that levels of benefits and allowances are adequate or that coverage is sufficient, however.

The amounts of social assistance allowances or social insurance benefits in the nine DMCs that had them in 2018 range from $79 to $4,395 per year per person with disabilities. As discussed in Chapter III on disability disaggregation, some of the higher-value benefits are linked to international programs.

The percentage of the population of people with disabilities that is being reached with disability-targeted allowances and benefits is not clear, as the reference population is not always established despite improvements in using standard instruments such as the WGQs in censuses and household surveys. In Nauru, for example, the 2019 census indicates a disability prevalence rate of 2.5% of the population, which

---

[107] Pacific Disability Forum. 2018. *Pacific Disability Forum SDG-CRPD Monitoring Report 2018—From Recognition to Realisation of Rights: Furthering Effective Partnership for an Inclusive Pacific 2030.* Suva. p. 5.

equates to 284 people with disabilities in 2018. Of these, 159 people receive the Disability Allowance in 2018, which represents 56% of the population of people with disabilities as defined in the census. It seems likely, however, that the census data are underestimating the number of people who have "a lot of difficulty" or "cannot do at all" in at least one domain of functioning, given the much higher disability prevalence rates that can be found in other Pacific DMCs and globally. The disability assessment mechanism in Nauru should also be noted as identifying only people who have very severe functional impairments. It is not aligned with the WGQs, the WHO Disability Assessment Schedule, or other instruments for identifying people with disabilities and assessing their functioning.

Expenditure on active LMPs is less than on social assistance and social insurance, but this is especially notable for the SPI for persons with disabilities. Many DMCs have policies that assume people with disabilities cannot work, and they are already excluded by multiple barriers from the labor market (footnote 107). Although the Pacific Framework for the Rights of Persons with Disabilities, 2016–2025 has a clear goal related to livelihood opportunities and inclusive employment for persons with disabilities, very few DMCs have developed government programs that contribute to achieving this goal. The Pacific Disability Forum noted, however, that more governments have been allocating funding for community-based rehabilitation and inclusive development services, such as Fiji, Kiribati, Solomon Islands, and Vanuatu. Across the region, such programs are essential for persons with disabilities and their families in rural, remote areas, and outer islands to access services and to foster stronger intersectoral collaboration. These programs have been instrumental in connecting persons with disabilities for livelihoods and technical and vocational education and training programs.

Conclusion

People with disabilities are among the poorest and most vulnerable people in the Pacific region. Disability prevalence increases with age, as functioning reduces. In some DMCs, more than half of all persons with disabilities are older than age 60 years. Most DMCs in the region have signed the CRPD, Incheon Strategy, and Pacific Framework for the Rights of Persons with Disabilities, 2016–2025 and are increasingly responsive to the needs of people with disabilities in social protection policies and programs. The Pacific Framework for the Rights of Persons with Disabilities, 2016–2025, sets out a subregional agenda that all of the DMCs that participated in the SPI study have endorsed and that further reinforces the implementation of the CRPD and Incheon Strategy.

It is likely that between 2009 and 2018, overall expenditure per GDP on disability-targeted programs increased slightly, albeit from a very low starting point. In seven Pacific DMCs, disability allowances have been introduced, but not all are universal or tailored to address the additional costs of disability. Only one program—in Fiji—can be combined with employment and other government welfare programs. The adequacy and coverage among people with disabilities of these allowances require further study. LMPs for people with disabilities require further strengthening across nearly all DMCs. There is a good example in Solomon Islands where community-based inclusive development programs are facilitating access to training, employment, and livelihood opportunities for people with disabilities both in disability-targeted and general programs. This initiative is mainly funded by donors and NGOs, although the government also contributes and coordinates.

All Pacific DMCs now use WGQs, designed to achieve more robust statistical estimates of disability prevalence, resulting in better prevalence data, but data collection for social protection administration still needs to improve, which will lead to better-tailored social protection programs. More disaggregated data collection is also needed to better understand how social protection programs and measures effectively complement each other to create more disability-inclusive social protection systems. Coverage of people with disabilities in general social protection programs, as well as CSO services and support programs funded by the government, should be tracked through administrative data and screening questions on functioning. This will result in more accurate reporting on social protection expenditures for people with disabilities than is currently possible.

Governments in the region tend to rely on development partners, NGOs, and CSOs to provide services and other support to people with disabilities. Only in a few DMCs is this support funded by government budgets or formally recognized in national policies and programs aimed at implementing the CRPD and supporting people with disabilities.

V. COVID-19: Socioeconomic Impacts and Social Protection Responses in the Pacific

The COVID-19 pandemic had profound negative economic and social impacts in the Pacific. The pandemic reduced employment and economic opportunities, eroded people's incomes and increased cost of living, and restricted access to education and health services. Across the region, these impacts have fallen disproportionately on vulnerable and marginalized groups—women, children, older people, youth, persons with disabilities, and persons living below nationally defined poverty lines.

This chapter first outlines the main economic and social impacts of COVID-19, before presenting the social protection measures Pacific DMCs have adopted to address these impacts. It also presents enterprise support measures that sought to help people maintain businesses and relieve pressures on livelihoods.

Economic and Social Impacts

While the Pacific DMCs have, in large measure, escaped the most severe health impacts of COVID-19, the very measures that led to this success—border closures and travel restrictions—have plunged the region into an economic crisis. For 2020–2021, the GDP across the region declined by almost 6%, albeit with significant intercountry variation. The Cook Islands took the hardest hit, with a GDP decline of almost 32%. Moreover, while most DMCs saw a drop in GDP, the smaller atoll countries—Kiribati, Nauru, and Tuvalu—saw modest growth over the same period.[108]

The decline of the tourism sector was one of the key drivers of economic downfall. In 2019, the Pacific region received almost 1.8 million visitors by air, 320,000 by sea, and an estimated $2.7 billion from these tourists. In 2020, these figures fell and continued to fall in 2021 due to border closures and reduction in travel. Across the region, arrivals in the first quarter of 2021 were 97.8% lower than arrivals in the first quarter of 2020.[109] The economic impact was especially severe in the six heavily tourism-based economies of the Cook Islands, Fiji, Niue, Palau, Samoa, and Vanuatu. In Fiji, by October 2020, 80% of tourism sector workers had lost their jobs.[110]

---

108 ADB. 2021. *GDP Growth in Asia and the Pacific: Asian Development Outlook (ADO)*. September. https://data.adb.org/dataset/gdp-growth-asia-and-pacific-asian-development-outlook (accessed 27 March 2022).

109 Pacific Tourism Organisation. Regional Tourism Resource Centre. https://southpacificislands.travel/.

110 Fiji Hotel and Tourism Association. https://fhta.com.fj/.

The fallout from this virtual cessation of tourism reverberated far beyond the industry, impacting agriculture, fisheries, wholesale and retail services, the informal sector, and government revenues. Vulnerable populations—women, informal workers, and employees from rural communities—were the most heavily impacted. For example, of the 26% of workers in Samoa who had lost their jobs by July 2020, 64% were women.[111] In Tuvalu, virtually the full impact on employment was borne by women.

The wholesale and retail sector across the Pacific region has been directly impacted by the shuttering of the tourism industry and by COVID-19 containment measures such as lockdowns, curfews, and regulation of operating hours. The sector has also been heavily impacted by wage and employment losses in the wider economy that translate into reduced household demand. Disruption of regional and global supply chains also negatively impacted operations, as have increased freight costs. In some cases, increases of up to 300% have been recorded, as shipping vessels operate on reduced schedules but with increased costs due to COVID-19 restrictions.[112]

The pandemic has impacted agriculture and food security in many ways. Across the region, demand has been reduced due to (i) suspension of tourism; closure of schools; and cancellation of social, cultural, business, and sporting events; and (ii) reduced household buying power due to wage and job losses. Lockdowns, restrictions on movement, suspension of public transport, closure of markets and prohibition of informal roadside markets, and social distancing have all acted as barriers to the flow of food from rural areas to urban centers. These same factors have, in turn, constrained the flow of staple foods (e.g., rice, sugar, and flour) from urban centers to rural areas, leaving many rural store shelves bare. These impacts have been felt most severely in those DMCs where a large proportion of the workforce is engaged in the informal sector and where child stunting was already prevalent before the pandemic.

The pandemic has disrupted fish supply chains in a manner similar to its impact on agriculture supply chains. It has reduced market opportunities, made it difficult to get fish to market and created labor shortages. Reduced global demand has created market uncertainty while increasing costs and reducing profitability. These factors translate into job losses in the domestic processing and support services that sustain offshore fishing fleets.[113]

---

[111] ILO. 2020. *ILO Brief: Findings of the Rapid Assessment (RA) in Fiji and Samoa*. https://www.ilo.org/wcmsp5/groups/public/---asia/---ro-bangkok/---ilo-suva/documents/publication/wcms_751883.pdf.

[112] K. Shen. 2020. *The Economic Costs of the Pandemic for the Pacific Islands*. Center for Strategic and International Studies. 9 September. https://www.csis.org/blogs/new-perspectives-asia/economic-costs-pandemic-pacific-islands.

[113] K. Shen. 2020. *The Economic Costs of the Pandemic for the Pacific Islands*. Center for Strategic and International Studies. 9 September. https://www.csis.org/blogs/new-perspectives-asia/economic-costs-pandemic-pacific-islands; and S. Sherzed. 2020. Impacts of COVID-19 on the Food Systems in the Pacific Small Island Developing States and Responses. *City Regions Food Systems Programme: Food and Agriculture Organization of the United Nations*. 1 June. https://www.fao.org/in-action/food-for-cities-programme/news/detail/en/c/1278570/.

People in the informal economic sector are disproportionately impacted by the loss of jobs and income. This impact was most acutely felt by women and youth, who primarily work in the informal sector in the Pacific. The informal sector makes an important contribution to the economies of all Pacific DMCs and is a significant source of employment—especially for women and youth. Pre-COVID-19, in Fiji, PNG, Solomon Islands, and Vanuatu, over 60.0% of the labor force was engaged in the informal sector. In Tonga, the rate was 77.9%. Although informal employment is generally lower in other Pacific DMCs, the informal sector remains a significant source of employment in virtually all DMCs, like the Cook Islands (28.7%), Kiribati (43.6%), the Marshall Islands (22.6%), and Samoa (37.3%).[114]

Many informal workers depend either directly or indirectly on the tourism economy and lost significant revenue when tourism was suspended. Other jobs that they most commonly hold—those in informal agriculture and handicrafts—were also among the first to disappear. Restrictions on mobility reduced opportunities for local sales, and the general economic contraction further depressed demand. In Fiji, 76% of persons employed in the informal sector say that their businesses are operating only partially, and their cash reserves to sustain operations will last for only a few months.[115] Informal sector enterprises established pre-COVID-19 also face new competition from persons entering the sector after losing their formal employment.

In most Pacific DMCs, women and youth do not have access to formal social protection or training opportunities as they mainly work in the informal sector. Women's economic vulnerability was compounded by restrictions on mobility and autonomy; increased unpaid caregiving responsibilities, including overseeing children learning remotely; and increasing rates of gender-based violence.

The worsening economic conditions that led to the loss of jobs, reduction in work hours, and falling revenue from self-employment and informal production negatively affected people's livelihoods across the region. These livelihood impacts can generally be quantified for the formal sector but only estimated for the informal sector.

(i)   In a survey conducted in the Cook Islands, 52.0% of the workforce reported losing income, including formal sector workers (49.5%), informal and casual workers (39.4%), and others (11.1%); of those losing income, 57.0% reported losing more than NZ$100 per day.[116]

(ii) In a survey conducted in Fiji, 50% of formal sector workers lost their jobs, and the majority who are still employed are working reduced hours.[117]

---

[114] ADB. Key Indicators Database. https://kidb.adb.org (accessed 27 March 2022); and ILO. ILOSTAT Database. https://ilostat.ilo.org/ (accessed 27 March 2022).

[115] UNDP. 2021. *Socio-Economic Impact Assessment of COVID-19 in Fiji*. Suva.

[116] United Nations Office of the Resident Coordinator for Cook Islands, Niue, Samoa, and Tokelau. 2020. *Socio-Economic Impacts of COVID-19 in the Cook Islands*. https://samoa.un.org/sites/default/files/2020-08/Cook%20Island%20socio%20economic%20impact.pdf.

[117] ILO. 2020. *ILO Brief: Findings of the Rapid Assessment (RA) in Fiji and Samoa*. https://www.ilo.org/wcmsp5/groups/public/---asia/---ro-bangkok/---ilo-suva/documents/publication/wcms_751883.pdf.

(iii)   In the Marshall Islands, 257 formal sector workers lost their jobs; there is no estimate of the impact on those working in the informal economy.[118]

(iv)   In the FSM, 504 formal sector workers lost their jobs; there is no estimate of the impact on those working in the informal economy.[119]

(v)   In Palau, 779 jobs were lost after adjusting for mitigation through a government-sponsored temporary work program; 25% of households reported COVID-19 losses in income derived from informal sector activities.[120]

(vi)   In Samoa, 50% of households reported that at least one member had lost their job, including in the formal sector (52%), informal and casual workers (40%), and other (8%).[121]

(vii)   In a 2021 survey across Melanesia, 58% of households have one or more household members who had lost their job or income, and 50% of households indicated that they can no longer meet normal household expenses.[122]

Loss of livelihoods is exacerbated by an increase in the cost of living. Between 2020 and 2021, food prices rose in PNG by 7.4%, in Solomon Islands by 4.2%, and in Vanuatu by 30.6% (footnote 122). In PNG, the cost of road transport also rose, in some cases doubling.[123] Rising transport costs are also contributing to reduced supplies of fresh food and staple root crops in urban areas and imported staples (i.e., flour, rice, sugar, and canned goods) in rural areas. In Melanesia, 50% of households reported that they are no longer able to meet normal expenses, leading some to reduce the quality or frequency of meals (25.0%), sell productive assets (14.5%), turn to begging or other high-risk activities (14.0%), or send their children to work (14.0%).[124]

[118]   EconMap. 2021. *The Economic Impact of COVID-19 on the Marshall Islands with Policy Options for Sustained Recovery*. Honolulu: PITI-VITI.

[119]   EconMap. 2021. *Assessing the Impact of COVID-19 on the FSM Economy*. Honolulu: PITI-VITI. https://pubs. pitiviti.org/fsm-covid-impact.

[120]   EconMap. 2021. *The Road to Recovery: Further Updating the Economic Impact of COVID-19 and Strategies for Mitigation in the Republic of Palau*. Honolulu: PITI-VITI. https://pubs.pitiviti.org/palau-covid-impact-update; and Palau Red Cross. 2020. *COVID-19 Household Assessment Report: Preliminary Results*. Koror.

[121]   United Nations Office of the Resident Coordinator for the Cook Islands, Niue, Samoa, and Tokelau. 2020. *Summary of the Samoan Rapid Socio-Economic Impact Survey for COVID-19. Socio-Economic Impact Assessment: Key Findings*. Apia. https://samoa.un.org/en/87285-summary-samoan-rapid-socio-economic-impact-survey-covid-19.

[122]   World Vision. 2021. *Pacific Aftershocks: Unmasking the Impact of COVID-19 on Lives and Livelihoods in the Pacific and Timor-Leste*. Melbourne.

[123]   J. Goro. 2020. The Impact of Coronavirus Pandemic on Access to Public Transportation in Papua New Guinea. PNG NRI *Spotlight*. 13 (8). https://pngnri.org.

[124]   World Vision. 2021. *Pacific Aftershocks: Unmasking the Impact of COVID-19 on Lives and Livelihoods in the Pacific and Timor-Leste*. Melbourne.

There is evidence of negative effects on food security and nutrition:

(i)   In Samoa, 57% of households lessened food consumption, while 46% reported eating cheaper, generally less nutritious meals.[125]
(ii)   In the Cook Islands, 33% were eating cheaper, less nutritious meals.[126]
(iii) In Melanesia, 50% of households could no longer afford a healthy diet, and 25% have shifted to lower-cost but less nutritious foods.[127]

Informal urban settlers were among the most affected. During pre-COVID-19, these residents had inequitable access to well-paying formal sector jobs and social protection, and many endured poor living conditions. As a result of the pandemic, settlement conditions have been accentuated by fewer livelihood opportunities. Unlike their rural counterparts, many in informal settlements are cut off from social support. Their proximity to ports of entry, coupled with poor access to safe water, sanitation, and hygiene facilities, increases their risk of contracting COVID-19. Poor housing conditions make lockdowns especially difficult, thus increasing the risk of family violence.

Children are impacted by household food insecurity as well as by school closures. School closures and introduction of distance learning education resulted in disruption of education and deterioration in the quality of schooling. These initial school closures lasted about 2–4 weeks in most DMCs. However, Fiji experienced the longest school closure, almost 1 year of learning split between two closure periods, one in 2020 (i.e., 3 months) and one in 2021 (i.e., 8 months). PNG, with over 14,000 schools and nearly 2.5 million students, was among the least prepared to support remote learning. There, provision of home-based schooling was challenging as a third of students did not have electricity at home and access to writing materials, and only 22% have access to radio or higher levels of technology.[128]

School closures had broader consequences for children. In the Pacific, as elsewhere in the world, schools provide not only education, but offer nutrition (through school lunches and in some places, breakfasts), provide child health screening and psychosocial support. School also offers opportunities for socialization, and pursuit of normal childhood activities including play, sports, and cultural expressions. The most vulnerable children, including those with disabilities were most affected

---

[125] United Nations Office of the Resident Coordinator for the Cook Islands, Niue, Samoa, and Tokelau. 2020. *Summary of the Samoan Rapid Socio-Economic Impact Survey for COVID-19. Socio-Economic Impact Assessment: Key Findings.* Apia. https://samoa.un.org/en/87285-summary-samoan-rapid-socio-economic-impact-survey-covid-19.

[126] United Nations Office of the Resident Coordinator for Cook Islands, Niue, Samoa, and Tokelau. 2020. *Socio-Economic Impacts of COVID-19 in the Cook Islands.* https://samoa.un.org/sites/default/files/2020-08/Cook%20Island%20socio%20economic%20impact.pdf.

[127] World Vision. 2021. *Pacific Aftershocks: Unmasking the Impact of COVID-19 on Lives and Livelihoods in the Pacific and Timor-Leste.* Melbourne.

[128] Government of PNG, National Department of Education. 2020. *COVID-19 Education Emergency Response and Recovery Plan.* Port Moresby. https://www.education.gov.pg/documents/PNG-COVID-19-Education-Response-and-Recovery-Plan-(Final-Draft-04-05-2020).pdf.

by the school closures. Remote learning modalities, at least in their initial phase, failed to consider the special needs of children with disabilities.

Negative health impacts from COVID-19 include actual morbidity and mortality, but there was also disruption of access to regular health services. Clinics are closed, canceled, or open for limited hours to reduce the risk of infection. Health workers have been reassigned to COVID-19 tasks (i.e., screening, testing, treating, and vaccination). Even where clinics operate normally, some—especially older persons and those with noncommunicable diseases—are reluctant to attend out of fear of infection. UNICEF reported a small downward trend in routine immunization caused by health worker redeployment; with evidence of increasingly poor diets, these have the potential to reverse recent gains in child health and nutrition.[129] Beyond this, few data exist to document the impacts of health systems preoccupied by COVID-19, some for extended periods of time.

Around the world, COVID-19 exacerbates mental health. The pathways for this impact are many—fear and uncertainty associated with the disease, stress from loss of income, the shift to less healthy meals, disrupted sleep, unhealthy coping mechanisms such as alcohol use, isolation from friends, absence from family, lack of pleasurable activities, increased caregiving burdens especially for women, and increased family- and gender-based violence. Mental health services across the Pacific region are underfunded and underdeveloped, and there is strong stigma associated with their use. There is some evidence of increasing levels of mental ill-health in Fiji and Vanuatu.[130]

Social Protection Response to COVID-19

In response to the economic and social consequences of the pandemic, the Pacific DMCs adopted a range of social protection measures. These measures include social insurance, social assistance, and labor market programs (Table 22).

1. Social Insurance

All Pacific DMCs have one or more contributory social insurance schemes; the most common are retirement benefit schemes. Several DMCs including the Cook Islands, Fiji, Palau, PNG, Samoa, Tonga, and Vanuatu assist individuals through waivers, deferrals, reductions, or subsidies of payments made by individuals into these schemes. In some DMCs, measures are applied widely (e.g., the Cook Islands and Fiji); in others, they are restricted to impacted sectors and/or individuals.

129 UNICEF Pacific. 2020. *2020 Country Office Annual Report*. Suva. https://www.unicef.org/media/101086/file/Pacific-Islands-2020-COAR.pdf.

130 WHO Regional Office of the Western Pacific. 2020. Mental Health in the Pacific. 10 October https://www.who.int/westernpacific/about/how-we-work/pacific-support/news/detail/10-10-2020-mental-health-in-the-pacific.

Table 22: Social Protection and Enterprise Support Measures Applied in the Wake of COVID-19

Measure		Countries
Social Insurance		
Unemployment benefits	Cash payments	Cook Islands, Fiji, Kiribati, Marshall Islands, FSM, Nauru, Palau, Samoa
	Disbursement from provident or other retirement funds	Fiji, Samoa, PNG, Solomon Islands
	Line of credit	PNG
	Cash for work	Palau
Waiver, delay, or subsidy for social security or pension fund payments due (individuals)		Cook Islands, Fiji, Palau, PNG, Samoa, Tonga, Vanuatu
Social Assistance		
Unconditional cash transfers to individuals and/or households		FSM, Nauru, Samoa, Solomon Islands, Tonga, Tuvalu
Utility subsidy or waiver (business or household)		Cook Islands, Fiji, FSM, Palau, Samoa, Solomon Islands, Tonga (note that Palau and Solomon Islands also subsidized internet)
Direct food support (in-kind assistance)		Fiji, Marshall Islands, Palau, Solomon Islands (2022 only)
Assistance (cash or in-kind) to vulnerable populations	Supplement to old-age benefits	Cook Islands, Nauru, Palau, Samoa, Tonga
	New or expanded child or student subsidies	Cook Islands, Fiji, Tonga, Tuvalu
	Assistance to pensioners, caregivers, infirm, destitute	Cook Islands, FSM, Nauru, Solomon Islands, Tonga
	Remote communities	Kiribati, Marshall Islands, Tuvalu
Sick leave payments for persons testing positive or required to isolate for COVID-19		Cook Islands, Fiji
Measures to address violence against women and/or children		Fiji, FSM, Palau, Tonga
Labor Market Programs		
Subsidies	Wage subsidies paid to employers to keep employees on the payroll or hire new employees	Cook Islands, Fiji, FSM, Samoa, Solomon Islands (public sector only), Tonga, Vanuatu
	Training subsidies	Cook Islands, Samoa
Employment services		Cook Islands, Nauru
Fiscal Measures Benefiting Businesses		
Direct support to business	Cash grants	Cook Islands, Fiji, Kiribati, Marshall Islands, FSM, Nauru, Palau, Samoa, Solomon Islands, Tonga, Vanuatu
	Loans to offset losses	Fiji, Palau, Solomon Islands, Tuvalu, Vanuatu, PNG
	Grants to support investment in primary sectors	Solomon Islands
	Support to micro, small, and medium-sized enterprises	Fiji, Kiribati, FSM, Solomon Islands, Tonga, Tuvalu
	Support to state-owned enterprises	Kiribati, Nauru, Solomon Islands, Vanuatu
	Subsidy for cash crop producers	Kiribati, Marshall Islands, Solomon Islands, Vanuatu
Tax and fee relief—waivers, delay, or subsidy for social security or pension fund payments (businesses)		Cook Islands, Fiji, FSM, Palau, PNG, Samoa, Solomon Islands, Tonga, Vanuatu
Food production (support for production—agriculture, gardening, fisheries)		Fiji, Kiribati, Marshall Islands, FSM, Palau, Solomon Islands, Tonga, Tuvalu, Vanuatu
Debt management assistance (e.g., repayment holidays and subsidies for interest)		Fiji, FSM, Palau, PNG, Samoa, Solomon Islands, Tonga, Tuvalu

continued on next page

Table 22: *continued*

Measure	Countries
Other Measures	
Assistance to citizens stranded overseas when borders closed (i.e., living subsidy and/or repatriation assistance)	Fiji, Kiribati, Marshall Islands, FSM, Nauru, Palau, Solomon Islands, Tonga, Tuvalu, Vanuatu
Export credit facility	Solomon Islands
Food security (support for production—agriculture, gardening, fisheries)	Fiji, Kiribati, Marshall Islands, FSM, Palau, Solomon Islands, Tonga, Tuvalu, Vanuatu
Investment in infrastructure to stimulate hiring	Solomon Islands, Vanuatu
Support to nongovernment organizations assisting with relief	FSM, Samoa
Social protection systems strengthening	Fiji
Relocation assistance (domestic)	Tuvalu, Solomon Islands (transport only)
Contingency plans for rationing food and fuel	Tuvalu
Price controls	Tuvalu

FSM = Federated States of Micronesia, PNG = Papua New Guinea.

Notes:
1. Niue is not included in this table due to lack of information.
2. Listed from most common to least common measures.

Sources: ADB. Cook Islands. ADB COVID-19 Policy Database. https://covid19policy.adb.org/policy-measures/COO (accessed 27 March 2022); ADB. Federated States of Micronesia. ADB COVID-19 Policy Database. https://covid19policy.adb.org/policy-measures/FSM (accessed 27 March 2022); ADB. Kiribati. ADB COVID-19 Policy Database. https://covid19policy.adb.org/policy-measures/KIR (accessed 27 March 2022); ADB. Marshall Islands. ADB COVID-19 Policy Database. https://covid19policy.adb.org/policy-measures/RMI (accessed 27 March 2022); ADB. Nauru. ADB COVID-19 Policy Database. https://covid19policy.adb.org/policy-measures/NAU (accessed 27 March 2022); ADB. Palau. ADB COVID-19 Policy Database. https://covid19policy.adb.org/policy-measures/PAL (accessed 27 March 2022); ADB. Papua New Guinea. ADB COVID-19 Policy Database. https://covid19policy.adb.org/policy-measures/PNG (accessed 27 March 2022); ADB. Samoa. ADB COVID-19 Policy Database. https://covid19policy.adb.org/policy-measures/SAM (accessed 27 March 2022); ADB. Solomon Islands. ADB COVID-19 Policy Database. https://covid19policy.adb.org/policy-measures/SOL (accessed 27 March 2022); ADB. Tonga. ADB COVID-19 Policy Database. https://covid19policy.adb.org/policy-measures/TON (accessed 27 March 2022); ADB. Tuvalu. ADB COVID-19 Policy Database. https://covid19policy.adb.org/policy-measures/TUV (accessed 27 March 2022); and ADB. Vanuatu. ADB COVID-19 Policy Database. https://covid19policy.adb.org/policy-measures/VAN (accessed 27 March 2022).

Prior to the COVID-19 pandemic, no Pacific DMC had a stand-alone contributory unemployment compensation fund, although the provident funds in Fiji and Solomon Islands allow members to withdraw from their accounts in the event of unemployment, thus addressing, in part, this gap in social protection.

Provident fund members have also been allowed to make withdrawals from or to take loans against their accounts such as in Fiji, PNG, Samoa, and Solomon Islands. In some countries, these benefits are one-time payouts designed to cushion the impact of abrupt unemployment (e.g., the Cook Islands paid 1 month of benefits at the minimum wage to individuals unemployed due to COVID-19). In others, benefits consist of continuing monthly payments (e.g., Palau, the FSM, and the Marshall Islands). Palau's COVID Response One-Stop Shop (CROSS) initiative has two options: cash benefits to the unemployed, or participation in a cash-for-work program. The cash-for-work program is managed by the Palau Visitors Authority, providing unemployed tourism sector workers with work in government or civil society with stipends paid from the CROSS initiative.[131] Palau appears to be the only Pacific DMC whose COVID-19 measures include a cash-for-work component.[132]

Eligibility for unemployment benefits vary. In some Pacific DMCs, eligibility is limited. In Nauru, for example, eligibility is limited to employees of Nauru Airlines. In most other DMCs, benefits are paid to workers in directly impacted industries, often defined as the tourism and hospitality industries. Workers in the formal sector are the primary beneficiaries. Those in the informal sector are either ineligible, as benefits are channeled through provident funds; or eligible for a limited one-time payment, as in Fiji, where licensed market venders in lockdown zones receive a one-time compensatory payout of F$150. In other DMCs, informal sector workers are technically eligible for benefits but often encounter difficulty in generating the required documentation for losses (e.g., Palau, the Marshall Islands, and the FSM). Kiribati prioritizes seafarers, fishery observers, fruit pickers, and casual workers in the construction and tourism industries for benefits, as these groups are unable to engage in their normal livelihoods due to border closures.

2.   Social Assistance

In the aftermath of the COVID-19 pandemic, several Pacific DMCs have expanded existing social assistance programs and established new—albeit mostly temporary— programs to assist those impacted by the economic downturn.

Unemployment assistance. Several DMCs such as the Cook islands, Fiji, the Marshall Islands, Nauru, Palau, the FSM, Samoa, Solomon Islands, Tonga, and Tuvalu—provide cash payments to certain categories of individuals or households. As in the case of unemployment benefits, these vary widely in scope (i.e., one-time payments versus continuing) and eligibility requirements (i.e., universal versus targeted).

As a combined economic stimulus and social assistance measure, Samoa provides a one-time payment of ST50 to every citizen. In addition to this universal measure, Samoa provides targeted cash benefits to households directly impacted by COVID-19 mitigation measures.[133] Similar needs-based support is provided to COVID-19-impacted households in Solomon Islands, where the economic assistance package also includes half-wage support for nonessential civil servants placed on leave to create fiscal space for COVID-19 response measures.[134] Like Samoa, Tuvalu also pays a universal benefit of A$40 per resident citizen; rather than a one-off stimulus, this is a monthly benefit that continues through the period of economic contraction.[135]

---

[131]   T. Remengesau. 2020. Signing Statement Re: HB 10-133-14, HD1, SD1, the Coronavirus Relief One Stop Shop Act. 27 April. https://www.palaugov.pw/wp-content/uploads/2020/04/RPPL-No.-10-56.pdf.

[132]   ADB. Tuvalu. ADB COVID-19 Policy Database. https://covid19policy.adb.org/policy-measures/TUV (accessed 27 March 2022).

[133]   ADB. Samoa. ADB COVID-19 Policy Database. https://covid19policy.adb.org/policy-measures/SAM (accessed 27 March 2022).

[134]   ADB. Solomon Islands. ADB COVID-19 Policy Database. https://covid19policy.adb.org/policy-measures/SOL (accessed 27 March 2022).

[135]   ADB. Tuvalu. ADB COVID-19 Policy Database. https://covid19policy.adb.org/policy-measures/TUV (accessed 27 March 2022).

In the wake of the COVID-19 pandemic, unemployment compensation under the US Coronavirus Aid, Relief, and Economic Security (CARES) Act was extended to citizens of freely associated countries in the North Pacific—Palau, the Marshall Islands, and the FSM.

These countries also have a significant number of noncitizen contract workers, most from Asia. Noncitizens are not eligible for CARES. To assist these workers, many of whom were stranded due to cessation of flights, Palau and the FSM used domestic resources to provide unemployment compensation to noncitizens unemployed or working reduced hours due to COVID-19. For example, the FSM's COVID-19 Pandemic Relief Program includes cash transfers to low-income households that do not benefit from CARES.[136]

Utility subsidies. The Cook Islands, Fiji, the FSM, Palau, Samoa, Solomon Islands, and Tonga assist households (and, in some cases, businesses) by reducing rates or providing subsidies for utilities. In Fiji, the FSM, Palau, and Solomon Islands, these benefits target low-income and vulnerable households. In Fiji, the FSM, and Palau, these measures are expansions of programs that preceded the pandemic. Only in the Cook Islands is the utility subsidy a universal—albeit temporary (3-month)—assistance measure. In a related measure, several DMCs, including Fiji and Palau, enacted a moratorium on utility disconnections during all or part of 2020.

Food assistance. Several DMCs including Fiji, the Marshall Islands, Palau, PNG, and Solomon Islands provide direct food assistance to impacted households. In Fiji and Palau, these are limited public–private partnerships organized in the early days of the pandemic when people were out of work, but formal government assistance programs had not yet begun. In the Marshall Islands and PNG, food assistance is part of the core government response.

In Fiji, two food assistance initiatives primarily serve tourism-dependent households in the Western Division. The Veilomani Food Bank Initiative was organized by the Fiji Competition and Consumer Commission, and is supported by the Australian High Commission, the embassies of Japan and the US, the private sector, and workers in selected government departments.[137] The Fiji CSO Alliance for COVID-19 Humanitarian Response organizes food banks and provides seedlings for home gardens, counseling support, and legal services to impacted households in the Western Division as well.[138]

In Palau, teachers and principals distributing student learning packets in the early days of the pandemic found households that were severely impacted by layoffs. The Ministry of Education, in partnership with the Palau Community Action Agency and assisted by community groups and private individuals, organized food baskets

---

[136]   ADB. Federated States of Micronesia. ADB COVID-19 Policy Database. https://covid19policy.adb.org/policy-measures/FSM (accessed 27 March 2022).

[137]   Fiji Competition and Consumer Commission. 2020. Veilomani Food Bank Initiative Established. *Fiji Sun*. 18 April. https://fijisun.com.fj/2020/04/18/veilomani-food-bank-initiative-established/.

[138]   I. Danford. 2021. CSO Alliance for COVID-19 Humanitarian Response Calls for Support of Struggling Fijians in the West. *Fiji Village*. 25 March. https://www.fijivillage.com/feature/CSO-Alliance-for-COVID-19-Humanitarian-Response-calls-for-support-of-struggling-Fijians-in-the-West-845xfr/.

for 235 households. The Palau Red Cross Society, also organizes distribution of fresh food to impacted households. These measures represent immediate humanitarian interventions pending the start of the government's flagship CROSS initiative.[139]

In the Marshall Islands, food baskets of rice, flour, sugar, and baking powder are provided to each outer island household for 6 months. This is contingency support should COVID-19 enter through one of the two ports of entry, Majuro or Kwajalein. In this eventuality, the containment plan calls for lockdown of the outer islands to prevent the spread to rural communities where health resources are limited. In PNG, food security activities, including distribution of food rations in the National Capital District during the early 2020 lockdown, were a part of the government's core early response package.[140] Food relief in Solomon Islands was not initiated until early 2022 in response to the spread of the Omicron variant. This initiative, organized by the Honiara City Council and Market Venders Association, provides food packets to households unable to shop due to lockdown measures.[141]

Assistance for older people. Several DMCs including the Cook Islands, Nauru, Samoa, and Tonga provide targeted assistance to older persons. In the Cook Islands, Nauru, and Samoa, this takes the form of one-time payments to pensioners. In Tonga, pension benefits have been increased without a cut-off date, suggesting that this measure may be permanent. Palau provides in-kind support to older persons in the form of hygiene kits. As part of the ADB COVID-19 response for affected poor and vulnerable groups, Palau will implement an integrated package of health, social, and environmental measures to assist homebound older people and persons with disabilities.[142]

Assistance for children. The Cook Islands provides a NZ$100 benefit for schoolchildren impacted by school closures for every fortnight that schools are closed. Tuvalu provides a subsidy of A$100 per month per student to all students overseas to relieve their families of a portion of their maintenance during the economic slowdown. Tonga provides a subsidy of T$110 per student per month to locally enrolled secondary school students to encourage them to stay in school rather than to drop out to join the labor force. In Fiji, pre-COVID beneficiaries of the Child Benefit received supplemental assistance as part of the COVID-19 response package, and with support from CSOs, school-feeding programs have been expanded. Tuition fee supplement of up to Vt42,000 per student was provided to students from early childhood education to secondary level in Vanuatu.

[139]   A. Tabelual. 2021. Personal communication; M. Sengebau. 2021. Personal communication; and L. Shiro. 2021. Personal communication.

[140]   U. Gentilini, M. Almenfi, I. Orton, and P. Dale. 2020. *Social Protection and Jobs Responses to COVID-19: A Real-Time Review of Country Measures.* Washington, DC: World Bank.

[141]   ADB. 2020. ADB Approves $16 Million Grant to Help Marshall Islands Fight COVID-19. News release. 1 December. https://www.adb.org/news/adb-approves-16-million-grant-help-marshall-islands-fight-covid-19.

[142]   ADB. Palau: COVID-19 Response for Affected Poor and Vulnerable Groups Project. https://www.adb.org/projects/54196-001/main#:~:text=not%20present%20%20%20Project%20Name%20%20,%20%20Grant%20%208%20more%20rows%20.

Assistance for other vulnerable groups. Caregivers of persons with disabilities or older persons are targeted for supplementary cash assistance in the Cook Islands. Persons with disabilities are targeted for cash assistance in Nauru and Tonga. In the FSM, vulnerable groups receive in-kind assistance in meeting medical and utility expenses and receive solar lamps. Information from Solomon Islands also indicates that cash assistance is provided to vulnerable groups.

Sick leave benefits. Fiji provides cash benefits (i.e., 21 sick days) to persons in the formal sector who test positive for COVID-19 and earn less than F$30,000 per year. For workers in the informal sector, a lump-sum benefit of F$1,000 is paid.[143] The Cook Islands pays minimum wage benefits for 14 days for workers ordered to self-isolate by the Ministry of Health, regardless of whether the employee ultimately tests positive.[144] These benefits are, in part, social assistance measures and, in part, incentives to encourage people to comply with medical orders. In a broader study of sick leave used as a tool for COVID-19 containment, ADB found that when combined with contact tracing and testing, these measures make significant contributions to reducing COVID-19 morbidity and mortality.[145] In Samoa, frontline health workers were also given assistance through cash payment when infected by COVID-19 or assistance to family beneficiaries in the event of death.

Assistance for outer islands. Several DMCs including Kiribati, the Marshall Islands and Tuvalu provide special assistance to outer island communities. The Kiribati COVID-19 support package includes specific provisions for the remote Line and Phoenix islands. The Marshall Islands provides every outer island household with a livelihood kit that includes essential food items together with equipment and supplies for agriculture and fisheries.

Several DMCs also have pursued active de-urbanization policies, assistance designed to incentivize the return of urban residents to their rural homes and to reduce the number of people at risk for contracting COVID-19, especially those living in informal urban settlements that typically lack safe housing and basic services. The assumption is that COVID-19 will enter first through the ports of entry in national capitals.[146] Other intended benefits are to reduce pressure for relief measures and to encourage increased economic productivity in agriculture and fisheries.

---

[143] Government of Fiji. 2021. *Pandemic Leave Policy.* http://www.oag.gov.fj/wp-content/uploads/2021/05/POL-44.2021-Pandemic-Leave-Policy-07.05.2021-updated-07052021.pdf.

[144] Government of the Cook Islands, Ministry of Internal Affairs. n.d. *Self-Isolation Support.* https://www.intaff.gov.ck/covid19-response-package/businesses/self-isolation-and-quarantine-cover/.

[145] G. Amoranto, R. Hasan, R. Larado, and D. Raitzer. 2020. Paid Sick Leave as a Tool for COVID-19 Control. *ADB Briefs.* No. 161. Manila: ADB. https://www.adb.org/sites/default/files/publication/661386/adb-brief-161-paid-sick-leave-covid-19-control.pdf.

[146] When COVID-19 hit Solomon Islands in January 2022, it came from cross-border (i.e., illegal) sea contact during a wedding feast between PNG and Ontong Java. Although health officials took prompt action to lock down Ontong Java when the first cases were discovered, action came too late. Cases had already spread to Honiara and elsewhere.

Tuvalu actively promotes de-urbanization by providing one-way transport subsidies for Funafuti residents to their home islands. To ensure that migrants are welcomed, fed, and housed until they can assimilate back into the community, the government also provides a subsidy to the outer island councils. In addition, the government opened several neighboring islets on the Funafuti atoll for residence. Almost 60% of Funafuti residents have taken advantage of the resettlement program.

Solomon Islands also actively encourages residents of Honiara to return to their home provinces. The government provides transport subsidies through grants of SI$250,000 to each parliamentarian to organize and to pay for the transport of their constituents. No funds were allocated to assist returning residents, as it is assumed that the customary *wantok* system will provide housing, food, and other essentials during the transition period.[147]

Addressing family- and gender-based violence. Several countries have taken concrete measures to address the issue of family and gender-based violence (GBV) as part of the COVID-19 response packages. Fiji created a COVID-19 Response Gender Working Group, and the FSM allotted funds to expand clinical services for victims of violence. Fiji and Tonga have classified domestic violence services as essential services, thus allowing counseling and shelters to continue to operate despite pandemic measures. Solomon Islands made available COVID-19 telephone GBV services in provinces. While Palau did not include family- and gender-based violence in its COVID-19 response package, it has worked with ADB to design interventions that will become operational in 2022 as part of the ADB-supported COVID-19 Response for Affected Poor and Vulnerable Groups Project.[148] Vanuatu will also implement multidisciplinary responses to GBV with focus on adolescents as part of ADB-supported COVID-19 Response for Affected Poor and Vulnerable Groups Project.

3.   Labor Market Programs

Several Pacific DMCs devised innovative strategies for channeling unemployment benefits to workers through their employers during the pandemic. The Cook Islands, Fiji, the FSM, Samoa, Solomon Islands, Tonga, and Vanuatu all encourage businesses to keep employees on board during the economic downturn and, in some cases, to hire new employees. Box 20 discusses the innovative approach used in the Cook Islands.

Complementing these schemes, the Cook Islands and Samoa provide subsidies to businesses to invest in training, taking advantage of the economic downturn as an opportunity to scale up the labor force. The Cook Islands and Nauru provide employment services to assist the unemployed in finding jobs.

Youth are receiving targeted assistance with employment opportunities in Fiji and Solomon Islands. In Tuvalu, they are targeted for training in traditional food production and preservation methods as a strategy for social integration and to enhance food security.

---

[147]   G. Nanau and M. Labu-Nanau. 2021. The Solomon Islands' Policy Response to COVID-19: Between Wontok and Economic Stimulus Package. *COVID-19 Social Policies Response Series.* No. 18. Bremen: CRC 1342.

[148]   ADB. Palau: COVID-19 Response for Affected Poor and Vulnerable Groups Project. https://www.adb.org/projects/54196-001/main.

Box 20: The Cook Islands—Sustaining the Private Sector during COVID-19

The Cook Islands COVID-19 response includes direct cash payments (i.e., social assistance) to households and certain categories of vulnerable persons. Regarding unemployment benefits, however, it has adopted an innovative approach that aims to prevent—rather than respond to—unemployment. Instead of paying an unemployment benefit to workers after they become redundant, the economic stimulus package pays benefits to employers to retain employees through the economic downturn. The subsidy, based on a 40-hour work week, pays NZ$320 per week for a full-time employee and NZ$160 per week for a part-time employee.

In this way, the same government payout serves two purposes—sustaining household incomes and sustaining business operations. This helps ensure that businesses are poised to quickly take advantage of short-term opportunities, such as the travel bubble with New Zealand, and to move efficiently and quickly to full operations when the pandemic subsides.

Businesses are further incentivized to combine the wage subsidy with a training subsidy designed to use the downturn as an opportunity to upskill the labor force. To qualify for the training subsidy, businesses are required to enroll their employees in a government-approved training program (i.e., the Cook Islands Technical Training Institute; University of the South Pacific, the Cook Islands Campus; or online). To qualify for the training grant, employees need to enroll in and complete certification. Once 75% of employees (Rarotonga businesses) or 50% of employees (outer island businesses) earn their certificate, businesses are eligible for a lump-sum payment of NZ$3,000 for businesses with a turnover of less than NZ$300,000; NZ$6,000 for businesses with a turnover between NZ$300,000 and NZ$5 million; and NZ$10,000 for businesses with a turnover greater than NZ$5 million. In this way, businesses are incentivized to retain employees while providing practical assistance to help them successfully complete their training courses.

Source: Government of the Cook Islands. 2020. *Phase II Fact Sheet: Wage and Training Support Initiative.* July. Avarua. http://www.mfem.gov.ck/images/_COVID19_ERP/Wage_and_Training_Subsidy_-_ERP_Phase_II.pdf.

4.   Fiscal Support to Enterprises

All Pacific DMCs provide support to businesses impacted by COVID-19 containment measures. The Cook Islands, Fiji, Kiribati, the FSM, the Marshall Islands, Nauru, Palau, Samoa, Solomon Islands, Tonga, and Vanuatu—provide cash grants directly to qualifying businesses to assist them in meeting the cost of staying in business. Box 21 discusses support to businesses in the FSM. While the main beneficiaries of these payments are formal sector businesses, several DMCs provide assistance to informal businesses even when they cannot meet the documentation standards required.

Box 21: Assisting Businesses in the Federated States of Micronesia

Businesses directly impacted by COVID-19 in the Federated States of Micronesia include hotels, handicraft vendors, beauty salons, travel agents, souvenir shops, shipping agents, tour operators, and taxi operators. These businesses are eligible for a one-time government economic relief payment in the amount of $900–$50,000. Informal businesses unable to present complete financial records are eligible for a flat rate of $900. Additional credit support is also made available for small businesses through the FSM Development Bank.

Source: ADB. Federated States of Micronesia. ADB COVID-19 Policy Database. https://covid19policy.adb.org/policy-measures/FSM (accessed 27 March 2022).

Fiji, Palau, PNG, Solomon Islands, Tuvalu, and Vanuatu offer loans to businesses at concessional rates to offset losses and to sustain operations.[149] Fiji expanded its Natural Disaster and Rehabilitation Facility (now the Disaster Rehabilitation and Containment Facility). Impacted businesses access these funds through commercial banks, credit institutions, or the Fiji Development Bank at a maximum interest rate of 5%.[150] Solomon Islands provides incentive grants to businesses investing in primary production sectors (i.e., agriculture, forestry, and fisheries) directly benefiting rural communities.[151] PNG provides a line of credit for selected businesses.[152] Tuvalu opened a loan window in the Development Bank of Tuvalu to expand credit options for businesses, including small and informal enterprises.[153] Vanuatu provides targeted assistance to the transport sector to support the movement of food and produce between Port Vila and Luganville and rural provinces.[154]

Several DMCs specifically target state-owned enterprises for assistance. Nauru's COVID-19 response package includes liquidity injections for Nauru Airlines and other state-owned enterprises to sustain their operations. Solomon Islands earmarked funds for equity investments in several state-owned enterprises, including SolTuna, Kolombangara Forest Products, and Solomon Airlines. Vanuatu provides subsidies to Air Vanuatu.

Fiji, Kiribati, the FSM, Tonga, and Tuvalu earmarked funds for micro, small, and medium-sized enterprises. Fiji devotes funds to assist pandemic unemployed persons to start up micro enterprises (Box 22). The FSM established a concessional line of credit through the FSM Development Bank to assist 200 small and medium-sized enterprises. In addition, Tonga expanded the pre-COVID government flagship loan scheme for micro, small, and medium-sized enterprises.

Several DMCs provide subsidies to cash crop producers. Kiribati and the Marshall Islands increased subsidized prices paid for copra; Solomon Islands subsidizes copra and cocoa; and Vanuatu subsidizes copra, kava, and cocoa, among other export crops.

The Cook Islands, Fiji, the FSM, Palau, PNG, Samoa, Solomon Islands, Tonga, and Vanuatu provide support to businesses in the form of waivers, delays, or subsidies for various taxes and fees, including licensure fees, import duties, and deposits to mandatory social insurance funds. Many businesses and individuals are unable to meet debt-serving obligations due to loss of income. Therefore, measures assist them

[149] ADB. ADB COVID-19 Policy Database. https://covid19policy.adb.org (accessed 27 March 2022).
[150] ADB. Fiji. ADB COVID-19 Policy Database. https://covid19policy.adb.org/policy-measures/FIJ (accessed 27 March 2022).
[151] ADB. Solomon Islands. ADB COVID-19 Policy Database. https://covid19policy.adb.org/policy-measures/SOL (accessed 27 March 2022).
[152] ADB. Papua New Guinea. ADB COVID-19 Policy Database. https://covid19policy.adb.org/policy-measures/PNG (accessed 27 March 2022).
[153] ADB. Tuvalu. ADB COVID-19 Policy Database. https://covid19policy.adb.org/policy-measures/TUV (accessed 27 March 2022).
[154] ADB. Vanuatu. ADB COVID-19 Policy Database. https://covid19policy.adb.org/policy-measures/VAN (accessed 27 March 2022).

Box 22: **Inclusive Economic Recovery through Sustained Enterprises in the Informal Economy of Fiji**

On 1 July 2020, the Fiji Trades Union Congress (FTUC) and the Fiji Commerce and Employers Federation, supported by the International Labour Organization, signed a memorandum of agreement jointly implementing their first COVID-19 recovery initiative, Transition to Business. The initiative targets redundant formal sector workers who have started potentially scalable businesses to build their capacities to sustain their micro businesses and income for their families. The medium- to long-term objective is for the targeted businesses to employ more unemployed workers and, through the private sector, contribute to economic recovery. Through the in-crisis rapid assessment, FTUC found that currently 50% of their surveyed members are unemployed; of these, 46% have ventured into self-employment. This includes farming, fishing, sewing, baking, and other micro businesses, and, as this is their first time in business, they need support to sustain their new jobs.

Source: ILO. 2020. Bipartite Initiative to Support Redundant Workers in Micro Businesses. News. 30 June. https://www.ilo.org/suva/public-information/WCMS_749600/lang--en/index.htm.

in debt management, including holidays on repayment and short-term subsidies for interest payments, as in Fiji, the FSM, Palau, PNG, Samoa, Solomon Islands, Tonga, and Tuvalu.

To enhance nutrition and food security at both the household and national levels while helping people reduce daily living expenses. DMCs like Fiji, Kiribati, the Marshall Islands, the FSM, Palau, PNG, Solomon Islands, Tonga, Tuvalu, and Vanuatu have invested in measures to increase domestic food production. In Vanuatu, the economic slowdown and aftermath of Cyclone Harold triggered a sharp rise in food prices of more than 30%. In response, the government earmarked 21% of the 2021 budget to boost production with an emphasis on fruit, vegetable, and commodity production. Urban gardening and aquaculture have also received support. Over 100 people participated in garden training in Port Vila, while government support in the form of fish fingerlings have been provided to backyard aquaculture producers who built their own fishponds.[155] In Palau, government and nongovernment agencies formed an urban garden consortium, providing assistance for food production to COVID-19-impacted households in Koror.[156]

5.   Civil Society and Social Solidarity Networks

All Pacific DMCs have extensive networks of faith-based, community-based, and nongovernment organizations that are helping people endure the COVID-19 crisis. In most, these groups are organized into a national association of NGOs, which, in turn, are members of the Pacific Island Association for NGOs that supports members with training and networking opportunities while providing an advocacy platform for civil

[155] Government of Vanuatu. 2020. *Vanuatu Recovery Strategy, 2020–2023*. Port Vila. https://reliefweb.int/report/vanuatu/vanuatu-recovery-strategy-2020-2023-tc-harold-covid-19-vanuatu-july-2020.
[156] C. Kitalong (College of Micronesia), F. Sengebau (Bureau of Agriculture), L. Basiluius (Palau Community Acton Agency), and others. Personal communications and unpublished meeting minutes.

society in the region. In many DMCs, representatives of civil society are part of the national emergency management networks that manage disaster risk assessments, preparation, and responses at the national level. The FSM and Samoa have explicitly recognized the important roles played by civil society by including direct support to these networks involved in COVID-19 relief measures as part of their socioeconomic recovery packages.

The pandemic prompted reinvigoration of traditional food systems and reemergence of cultural safety nets, including modernization of some cultural systems such as bartering.[157] Box 23 discusses the practice of bartering based on local solidarity and mutual assistance.

Box 23: Nurturing a Community of Kindness through Bartering

In Pacific cultures, barter systems have long been a currency for exchanging goods and services. Over time, bartering has become rare, at least in urban centers, where people generally use cash to purchase goods and services. However, this traditional system reemerged on a large scale in Fiji in 2020, during the first wave of the COVID-19 outbreak. Marlene Dutta, administrator for the Barter for Better Fiji Facebook group, explained the concept at the 2021 Pacific Resilience meeting:

> The year 2020 really was an uncertain time. We had just closed our borders, thousands of people were out of employment, so I sat down, and I asked myself the question: What would happen if money ran out? One of the answers for me was, bartering . . . We had all the right ingredients for barter to flourish. We had people who were familiar with it. We had the platform to make barter easier to use in today's world, and all the other components that would really make bartering a solution to what we were going through in terms of job losses.

The Facebook group allows members from across Fiji to trade commodities they have in their home, including goods that they could grow, catch, and harvest. Dutta explained that this platform gained momentum in Fiji at a time when "people were watching what they were spending and needed to keep cash for their rent, their bills. This Facebook group offered them a space to be able to trade, to save their cash for those purposes and trade things they had for what they needed."

The Barter for Better Fiji Facebook group currently has close to 200,000 members actively exchanging goods and services in the country. The page has become so popular that sister pages have popped up in other countries, including Solomon Islands.

Source: SPC. 2021. Bartering through the Pandemic in Fiji. Web Stories. 29 November. https://www.spc.int/updates/blog/2021/11/bartering-through-the-pandemic-in-fiji.

---

[157] V. Iese et al. 2021. Impacts of COVID-19 on Agriculture and Food Systems in Pacific Island Countries: Evidence from Communities in Fiji and Solomon Islands. *Agriculture Systems.* 190.

VI. Future Directions for Social Protection in the Pacific

Introduction

The past 2 decades have seen governments across the Pacific recognize the potential of social protection instruments to reinforce community-based mechanisms for tackling hardships and risks that their populations face, particularly in the era of increasingly severe natural, epidemiological, and economic shocks. The associated vulnerabilities have often reflected inadequate access to social services and limited economic prospects rather than income poverty or basic goods deprivation, highlighting the importance of integrated and comprehensive social protection responses.

Pacific DMCs face significant challenges but also unique opportunities to channel the impacts of the COVID-19 pandemic into strategies that will build resilience and lead to development. Some of these DMCs are confronting fragile contexts, and new social protection initiatives can offer prospects to strengthen government service delivery and consolidate social contracts that build state credibility and reinforce demand for good governance. The Pacific's most promising social protection directions will better enable governments to invest in human and cognitive capital, develop productive opportunities for youth, and optimize a mix of climate and development strategies that will build green and sustainable societies and economies.

This chapter assesses historical trends in Pacific DMCs and identifies several key directions in the evolution of national social protection systems. The next section analyzes the longer-term social protection patterns and trends through 2019, laying the foundations for the subsequent analysis. The subsequent section discusses the impact of the COVID-19 pandemic on these developments, documenting the powerful effect of the epidemiological, economic, social, and political shocks. The main section then maps out seven future directions for social protection in Pacific DMCs, documenting trends in successes and identifying critical areas for future progress. The final section concludes with key lessons for governments and their development partners for the future of social protection in the Pacific.

Pre-COVID-19 Trends and Strategic Directions in Social Protection

Historically, Pacific DMCs developed a diverse set of social protection systems across the region. Through its SPI reports, ADB has concluded that these formal social protection systems rely heavily on contributory social insurance and provident funds, benefiting mainly those in the public sector, with significant gaps in social assistance for the most vulnerable.[158] Upper-income DMCs, such as the Cook Islands, provide life-cycle benefits for the vulnerable (including child benefits, caregiver allowances, destitute and infirm persons relief, social pensions, and disability grants). However, lower middle-income DMCs usually offer limited social assistance benefits. In addition, most Pacific DMCs primarily rely on traditional and informal social protection systems—the *wantok* system in PNG, for instance, provides a kinship-based form of traditional social protection, but urbanization, the monetization of the local exchange economy, and increasingly pervasive community-wide and national and international (covariate) shocks have stressed its adequacy and effectiveness.[159] Similar challenges have affected Solomon Islands and Tonga, compounded by tensions between market-oriented development initiatives and traditional systems of social support.[160]

The global economic crisis in 2008 triggered the first regionally coordinated impetus to strengthen government-funded social protection initiatives in the Pacific. The crisis coincided with climate and epidemiological shocks in a number of Pacific DMCs, exacerbating co-vulnerabilities that had already strained traditional support systems.[161] Indeed, several Pacific DMCs are ranked as the most vulnerable countries in the world facing climate shocks.[162] Repeated shocks undermine the resilience of households and often exacerbate debt traps. In Samoa, some employees expended their entire salary repaying their debts.[163]

As such, governments in the Pacific have progressively innovated and expanded formal social protection systems. From 2010, a limited number of social assistance programs began to support vulnerable households in the Pacific, such as social pensions in the Cook Islands, Fiji, Kiribati, Nauru, Niue, Samoa, and Tuvalu.[164] Fiji reformed the Family Assistance Program—the nation's main social assistance scheme reaching poor households—and the Cook Islands, Fiji, one island in Nauru, and New Ireland Province in PNG delivered a noncontributory disability pension.

[158] ADB. 2012. *The Revised Social Protection Index: Methodology and Handbook.* Manila; and ADB. 2016. *The Social Protection Indicator: Assessing Results for the Pacific.* Manila.

[159] For further analysis of how traditional support systems have weakened, see M. Chung. 2010. *Weaving Social Safety Nets in the Pacific. Pacific Studies Series.* Manila: ADB; M. Samson and D. Amosa. 2012. *Samoa Country Case Study.* Canberra: AusAID; N. Freeland and K. Robertson. 2010. *Vanuatu Country Case Study.* Canberra: AusAID; R. Slater. 2011. *Solomon Islands Country Case Study.* Canberra: AusAID; F. Ellis. 2012. Informal Social Protection in Pacific Island Countries—Strengths and Weaknesses. *AusAID Pacific Social Protection Series: Poverty, Vulnerability and Social Protection in the Pacific.* Canberra: AusAID.

[160] A. Ross and K. Bryceson. 2019. Traditional Thinking: The Impact of International Aid on Social Structures and Cultural Traditions in Agrifood Chains in Tonga and Solomon Islands. *Journal of the Asia Pacific Economy.* 24 (3). pp. 402–429.

[161] For discussions of interacting shocks in PNG and Samoa, see M. Samson. 2009. *Cash Transfers to Improve the Protection and Care of Vulnerable Children and to Empower Families in the Context of the HIV Epidemic in Papua New Guinea: Conceptual Framework.* Port Louis: Department for Community Development, Institute of National Affairs, and UNICEF. http://www.inapng.com/pdf_files/Social%20Cash%20 Transfers%20-Concept%20-Samson%20UNICEF-INA-DfCD.pdf; and M. Samson and D. Amosa. 2012. *Samoa Country Case Study.* Canberra: AusAID.

[162] The countries with the highest disaster risk worldwide are Vanuatu (47.73), Solomon Islands (31.16), and Tonga (30.51). M. Aleksandrova, et al. 2021. *World Risk Report 2021.* Berlin: Bündnis Entwicklung Hilf.

[163] M. Samson and D. Amosa. 2012. *Samoa Country Case Study.* Canberra: AusAID.

[164] In Fiji, food vouchers amount to F$30 for those older than age 70 years; in Kiribati, A$40 per month for those ages 67 years and older, increasing to A$50 after age 70 years; and in Samoa, ST55 for those ages 65 years and older. There are disability grants in Nauru and the Cook Islands, and a child benefit up to age 12 years in the Cook Islands.

In 2016, Cyclone Winston—the most intense tropical cyclone currently on record in the Southern Hemisphere—further challenged governments and their development partners to integrate shock-responsive approaches into integrated social protection and disaster management systems.[165] The World Bank, ADB, and DFAT thus worked to expand social protection support, providing the financial and technical resources to enable more effective and shock-responsive systems. When Cyclone Gita struck Tonga in 2018—the worst storm in the country's history—social protection responses, including cash transfers, were able to be rolled out within weeks. The Government of Tonga delivered almost T$1 million through two core social protection programs—the Social Benefits Scheme for the Elderly and Disability Benefits Scheme.[166] While this vertical expansion enabled a rapid response for existing beneficiaries, however, it excluded many vulnerable people affected by the disaster but not covered by existing programs.

The Pacific region has also witnessed its social assistance programs expanding greatly over the past decade. The increasing need for social assistance reflects the long-term trend of the importance of markets in allocating resources and in meeting the basic needs of the population. Rising urbanization contributes to the expanded role of markets while exposing the challenge of unemployment, particularly for youth who are more likely to migrate from rural areas to cities and to face greater challenges in finding work. The Pacific region has urbanized rapidly, and a majority of the population now lives in cities, highlighting the gap in urban social protection delivery.[167]

Demographic changes further challenge the foundations of Pacific economies. Changing fertility patterns, greater life expectancy, and increased migration all contribute to rising dependency ratios that stress limited livelihood opportunities. These long-term trends test the effectiveness and sustainability of traditional and informal support networks and systems, which often can effectively address individual (i.e., idiosyncratic) shocks but often prove inadequate in the face of community-wide, national, and global (i.e., covariate) crises.

Despite the rapid expansion of social assistance, gaps persist. In some Pacific DMCs, political interests have motivated the multiplication of schemes without adequate analysis of poverty and vulnerability. These fragmented systems often neglect the most vulnerable groups that lack sufficient voice or political constituency. A United Nations report identified fragmentation as a major challenge, complicated by the manner in which schemes are managed by diverse authorities, with varying

---

[165] Shock-responsive social protection systems anticipate and respond to a range of social, economic, epidemiological, natural, and political shocks and enable timely interventions that can scale up and adapt as necessary to tackle the multidimensional facets of complex and cascading crises. Shock-responsive systems increasingly integrate climate, development, humanitarian, and equity strategies. Shock-responsive systems involve multiple kinds of expansions: (i) vertical expansions increase benefits for existing beneficiaries, (ii) horizontal expansions increase coverage to new beneficiaries, and (iii) intersector expansions integrate complementary investments to strengthen developmental synergies.

[166] J. Doyle. 2018. Manna from Heaven—Cyclones, Cash Transfers, and the Role of Social Protection in Disaster Response. DevPolicyBlog. 20 March. https://devpolicy.org/cyclones-cash-transfers-and-the-role-of-social-protection-in-disaster-response-20180320/.

[167] The Pacific's largest country—PNG—remains overwhelmingly rural. World Bank. Urban Population (% of population)—Pacific Small Island States. https://data.worldbank.org/indicator/SP.URB.TOTL.IN.ZS?locations=S2 (accessed 12 May 2022).

histories, mandates, organizational cultures and reporting lines, and social protection views.[168] As of 2021, only the Cook Islands and Fiji provide established systems with significant cash transfer benefits for vulnerable children.

As previously discussed, contributory social insurance programs represent the largest share of government investments, but these usually only reach small proportions of workers (and their families) in the formal sector. These programs often incorporate provident funds for retirement, which provide limited long-term income security and inadequate protection against disability. Moreover, permanent old-age income security is inadequate, because the majority of provident fund beneficiaries choose lump-sum payments rather than annuities.

Pacific DMCs also have a range of LMPs. Some offer public works schemes and other benefits linked to the provision of labor. The cost of Kiribati's copra subsidies, a system of incentives with multiple social and economic objectives, rose from 8% of GDP in 2004 to an estimated 12% in 2017, with projections falling to 11% in 2021.[169]

Historically, the Pacific region's social protection systems have faced significant evidence gaps informing social protection policy development compared with other regions of the world.[170] In recent years, investments by ADB, the World Bank, DFAT, and United Nations agencies have expanded research and strengthened evidence-informed policy development. This research has contributed to a shift in thinking about poverty and vulnerability in the Pacific, highlighting the increasing risks from escalating shocks, particularly those stemming from climate change.

Lessons from COVID-19 Responses for Future Trends in Social Protection

The global COVID-19 pandemic triggered changes to the shock-responsive approach of many Pacific DMCs. Even in the absence of COVID-19 cases, most have imposed states of emergency, travel bans, and other measures that accelerated and intensified

---

[168] ILO Regional Office for Asia and the Pacific. 2020. *Social Protection Responses to COVID-19 in Asia and the Pacific: The Story So Far and Future Considerations*. https://www.ilo.org/wcmsp5/groups/public/---asia/---ro-bangkok/documents/publication/wcms_753550.pdf.

[169] The World Bank described the copra subsidy as "an agricultural subsidy to maintain copra production (a key export), a cash transfer to ensure a supply of cash in outer islands to maintain a monetized economy, an unemployment benefit to provide cash incomes to those who would otherwise be unemployed, a form of conditional cash transfer to encourage people to remain on the outer islands in order to slow urban migration, and one of the key transfer mechanisms that the government uses to redistribute its rising resource wealth (fishing license fee revenue) to the population of the outer islands." World Bank. 2018. *International Development Association Program Document for a Proposed Development Policy Grant in the Amount of SDR 3.6 Million (US$ 5 Million Equivalent) to the Republic of Kiribati for the Fifth Economic Reform Development Policy Operation*. Washington, DC.

[170] For example, a review found no rigorous impact assessments of national social protection programs in the Pacific and limited evidence on schemes at subnational levels. In contrast, extensive volumes of research have documented impacts of programs in Latin America, Africa, and Asia, often supported by integrated regional evidence-building initiatives. EPRI. 2022. *Policy Brief on Social Protection Regional Evidence Initiatives*. Cape Town.

the livelihood shock while providing a broad measure of epidemiological protection. Global and national policy responses decimated tourism throughout the region, and the economic shock diminished remittances, key elements of many GDPs and household budgets.

Some Pacific DMCs—including the Cook Islands, Fiji, Samoa, Solomon Islands, Tonga, Tuvalu, and Vanuatu—vertically expanded their social protection benefits as a preemptive response on an unprecedented scale, supporting households in complying with public health measures and enabling them to better cope with the livelihood shock.[171] In many, the COVID-19 crisis did not launch the momentum for social protection but rather accelerated the pace of developments initiated in prior years. For example, Kiribati added significant top-ups as a pandemic response to a support fund for unemployed workers, vertically expanding initiatives that pre-date the crisis. The Cook Islands provided a NZ$100 fortnightly cash benefit to all children up to age 16 years, vertically and horizontally expanding an existing child allowance.[172]

The pandemic also motivated demand to create social protection policies, strategies, and frameworks throughout the region. In PNG, the Department for Community Development, with support from ADB and the World Bank, initiated a new process to develop a national social protection policy. Similarly, the Government of Nauru, with ADB support, developed a national social protection strategy. The governments of Kiribati, Samoa, the Cook Islands, and Tuvalu enlisted UNICEF to support the development of national social protection policies and legislation.[173] A joint United Nations program is providing similar support to the Government of Samoa to develop a national social protection strategy.[174]

While around the world, social assistance measures dominate national responses, several Pacific DMCs like the FSM, the Marshall Islands, PNG, Samoa, Tonga, and Tuvalu mainly rely on cash transfers, fee waivers, service subsidies, and other social assistance measures to reach those affected by the crisis. The Government of PNG, with support from the World Bank and funding from DFAT, is piloting a nutrition-sensitive social protection program that includes cash transfers for children,

---

[171]   UNICEF. 2020. Strengthening Social Protection Systems to Respond to Compounding Shocks during Covid-19. https://www.unicef.org/pacificislands/media/2361/file/Strengthening%20Social%20 Protection%20Systems%20to%20Respond%20to%20Compounding%20Shocks%20during%20 COVID-19.pdf.

[172]   Government of the Cook Islands, Ministry of Internal Affairs. School Closure Support. https://www.intaff. gov.ck/covid19-response-package/family-elderly-children/school-closure-support/.

[173]   UNICEF. 2020. Strengthening Social Protection Systems to Respond to Compounding Shocks during Covid-19. https://www.unicef.org/pacificislands/media/2361/file/Strengthening%20Social%20 Protection%20Systems%20to%20Respond%20to%20Compounding%20Shocks%20during%20 COVID-19.pdf.

[174]   The Universal Social Protection Programme is a joint initiative by the United Nations through the Joint SDG Fund and is implemented by UNDP, UNESCO, ILO, UNESCAP, and UNICEF. S. Marinescu. 2021. Strengthening Resilience of Pacific Island States through Universal Social Protection: Presentation for the Pacific Forum on Sustainable Development. 25 November. Coral Coast, Fiji. https://www.unescap.org/ sites/default/d8files/event-documents/04.%20Session%202b_Strengthening%20Resilience%20of%20 PIS_Samoa%20UNRC.pdf.

motivated in part by the COVID-19 pandemic.[175] Samoa provides a universal cash benefit of ST50 to all citizens, new and expanded pension benefits for older people, housing benefits, utility subsidies, tax reductions on basic foods, and support to NGOs reaching vulnerable groups during the pandemic. Others, including the Cook Islands, Palau, and Vanuatu, are implementing stimulus packages that include social assistance measures for workers and vulnerable groups along with support for affected businesses.

Pacific DMCs also rely on LMPs for their social protection responses during the pandemic, including subsidies to firms to retain and to retrain their workers, as well as production subsidies for smallholder farmers. For example, the Cook Islands provides unemployment benefits as well as support for businesses and sole traders demonstrating negative impacts from the economic crisis, in addition to training grants to upskill workers and to increase their productivity. The Government of Solomon Islands developed the Economic Stimulus Package program, with provisions to support people's basic livelihoods, provide tax benefits to bolster employment, and increase subsidies for copra and cocoa to strengthen rural areas facing reverse migration in response to the economic shock.[176]

In addition, Vanuatu has implemented an employment stabilization fund to support firms to maintain their workforce; grants for micro, small, and medium-sized enterprises; and price subsidies and other support for smallholder farmers. Many Pacific DMCs are also using other types of instruments. The Cook Islands provides an immediate additional NZ$400 social assistance benefit, using a bank account transfer to existing social assistance beneficiaries, school closure support payments for children on Rarotonga, electric bill subsidies, and grants for families demonstrating economic hardship as a consequence of the pandemic. Vanuatu provides school fee waivers.[177]

Fiji and Palau have adapted their social insurance programs to deliver shock-responsive benefits to the crisis, while Tuvalu and Samoa include these as major tools alongside their primary interventions.[178] Samoa has sanctioned a 6-month moratorium on pension contributions for the hospitality sector.[179] The Cook Islands has reduced superannuation fund contribution requirements. However, DMCs like Fiji and Vanuatu that have allowed individuals to tap provident

[175]   World Bank. Child Nutrition and Social Protection Project. https://projects.worldbank.org/en/projects-operations/project-detail/P174637.

[176]   G. Nanau and M. Labu-Nanau. 2021. The Solomon Islands' Policy Response to COVID-19: Between Wantok and Economic Stimulus Package. *COVID-19 Social Policies Response Series*. No. 18. Bremen: CRC 1342.

[177]   U. Gentilini et al. 2022. Social Protection and Jobs Responses to COVID-19: A Real-Time Review of Country Measures. Washington, DC: World Bank. https://openknowledge.worldbank.org/handle/10986/37186; UNICEF. 2020. *Strengthening Social Protection Systems to Respond to Compounding Shocks during COVID-19*. https://www.unicef.org/pacificislands/media/2361/file/Strengthening%20Social%20Protection%20Systems%20to%20Respond%20to%20Compounding%20Shocks%20during%20COVID-19.pdf; and N. Tirivayi et al. 2020. A Rapid Review of Economic Policy and Social Protection Responses to Health and Economic Crises and Their Effects on Children: Lessons for the COVID-19 Pandemic Response. *Innocenti Working Papers*. New York: UNICEF.

[178]   N. Carandang and N. Del Castillo. 2020. Social Protection and COVID-19 in the Pacific: Economic Inoculation to Mitigate the Impacts of the Pandemic. In ADB. *Pacific Economic Monitor*. Manila. December. pp. 33–36.

[179]   U. Gentilini, M. Almenfi, I. Orton, and P. Dale. 2020. *Social Protection and Jobs Responses to COVID-19: A Real-Time Review of Country Measures*. Washington, DC: World Bank.

funds for emergency benefits may struggle to sustain these benefits and face increasing pressures on old-age income insecurity in the future.

Indeed, the COVID-19 crisis has led to unprecedented fiscal expansions that threaten the sustainability of these ambitious measures. Discussions with experts have highlighted concerns about the fiscal sustainability of the vertical and horizontal expansions of social protection systems across the region. The Government of Palau, for example, has announced measures amounting to $20 million (8% of GDP) to mitigate the negative economic and social impact, including an unemployment benefits scheme, temporary expansions to existing subsidies for utility bills, and a short-term job creation scheme for public works (footnote 140). These challenges of fiscal sustainability are compounded when financed through borrowing, highlighting the importance of new initiatives for domestic resource mobilization.

While the substantial increases of 2020–2021 may diminish as the crisis subsides—in line with the logic of shock-responsive expansions and contractions—the COVID-19 pandemic has demonstrated the power of social protection to adapt to protect the newly vulnerable from shocks. Continued development partner support may bridge the gap until domestic resource mobilization can finance the necessary systems. DFAT has supported PNG with A$30 million to support school fee waivers, as the government renewed its commitment to a tuition-free policy in the face of pandemic-related drops in school attendance. DFAT is also planning an additional A$35 million investment to sustain this initiative.

The COVID-19 pandemic has strengthened political will for social protection along multiple dimensions. The universal nature of the shock has created an impetus for more universal responses. Tuvalu attracted global attention when it implemented the universal Emergency Basic Income for its entire population.[180] The government delivered a cash transfer of A$40 per person to everyone in Tuvalu in both April and May 2020 and then is targeting individuals without regular income from June 2020.[181] The pandemic has expanded social protection's convening power, attracting the attention of policy stakeholders that have historically ignored the social protection sector.

Seven Future Directions for Social Protection in the Pacific

1.   Improving Coverage of Vulnerable Groups

A positive trend—and future direction—for social protection in the Pacific involves the progressive expansion of coverage of vulnerable groups. Pacific DMCs have expanded social pensions, disability grants, child benefits, and other programs that

---

[180]   M. Torry. 2020. Emergency Basic Income in Tuvalu. Basic Income Earth Network. 9 June. https://basicincome.org/news/2020/06/emergency-basic-income-in-tuvalu/.
[181]   ADB. 2020. *Pacific Economic Monitor*. Manila. December.

cover more of the population. Discussions with policy makers and key stakeholders in the region indicate that this trend is likely to continue, as a response to climate change and disaster risks and how COVID-19 exacerbated difficulty and vulnerability to a scale not previously experienced in the region.

In the past 15 years, the Cook Islands, Fiji, Nauru, Tonga, and Tuvalu have adopted social protection schemes for people with disabilities, while the Cook Islands, Fiji, Kiribati, Nauru, Niue, and Samoa have implemented universal old-age pensions.[182] Fiji plans to expand social protection support for vulnerable groups, as its latest national development plan indicates that "targeted social protection will continue to be provided for the vulnerable through new initiatives."[183] Indeed, with support from the Government of Australia, it has expanded social assistance benefits to tackle vulnerability, building on commitments entrenched in its national disability and gender policies.[184] Tonga has also improved the shock-responsiveness of its national disability benefit scheme, expanding benefits in the aftermath of Cyclone Gita, as discussed previously.[185] Tonga also increased social pension benefit to those aged 80 years and older.[186] These benefits proved vital in strengthening resilience to the economic consequences of the COVID-19 pandemic.[187]

As studies reported that about two-thirds of those ages 60 years and older in Vanuatu continue to work—mainly due to lack of retirement income security—the national sustainable development plan has made improved coverage of vulnerable groups, such as older persons, a core policy objective.[188] In Samoa, more than one-half of people with disabilities have no education and most children with disabilities faced severe challenges in accessing schooling.[189] However, in 2021, the government announced new measures "to ensure that persons with disabilities can access social protection measures."[190] The program is still pending implementation, but discussions with experts have confirmed the durability of these developments.

[182] Pacific Disability Forum. 2018. *Pacific Disability Forum SDG-CRPD Monitoring Report 2018—From Recognition to Realisation of Rights: Furthering Effective Partnership for an Inclusive Pacific 2030.* Suva.

[183] Government of Fiji. 2017. *Twenty-Year Development Plan 2017–2036.* https://www.adb.org/sites/default/files/linked-documents/LD4%205yr%20and%2020yr%20DP%20Transforming%20Fiji.pdf.

[184] Fiji National Council for Disabled Persons and Government of Fiji, Ministry of Health, Women and Social Welfare. 2008. *Fiji Islands: A National Policy on Persons Living with Disabilities, 2008–2018.* Suva. https://planipolis.iiep.unesco.org/sites/default/files/ressources/fiji_2008-18_nationaldisabilitypolicy.pdf; and Government of Fiji, Ministry of Social Welfare, Women, and Poverty Alleviation. 2014. *Fiji National Gender Policy.* Suva. http://extwprlegs1.fao.org/docs/pdf/fij171550.pdf.

[185] D. Larasati, K. Huda, A. Cote, S. Rahayu, and M. Siyaranamual. 2019. Inclusive Social Protection for Persons with Disability in Indonesia. *TNP2K Policy Briefs.* January. http://www.tnp2k.go.id/download/65217190113-PB%20DisabilitiesEng-web.pdf.

[186] Socialprotection.org. Social Welfare Scheme. https://socialprotection.org/discover/programmes/social-welfare-scheme (accessed 12 May 2022).

[187] UNPRPD. 2020. Initial Overview of Specific Social Protection Measures for Persons with Disabilities and Their Families in Response to COVID 19 Crisis. Draft. https://unprpd.org/sites/default/files/Overview%20response_1.4.pdf.

[188] N. Freeland and K. Robertson. 2010. *Vanuatu Country Case Study.* Canberra: AusAID.

[189] M. Samson and D. Amosa 2012. *Samoa Country Case Study.* Canberra: AusAID.

[190] M. Membrere. 2021. New Funding Disability Advocates' "Dream." *Samoa Observer.* 14 October. https://www.samoaobserver.ws/category/samoa/93036#:~:text=%22And%20it%20is%20actually%20a,the%20funding%20will%20be%20distributed.%22.

Governments are working to extend the coverage of contributory programs to the more vulnerable in the informal sector as well, but success and sustainability depend on robust institutional arrangements. Although Pacific DMCs are expanding programs for people with disabilities, data gaps threaten to limit the scaling up and monitoring of existing initiatives.[191] Statistical agencies are introducing the WGQs to improve the evidence base, but continued efforts toward data gathering and monitoring are required.[192]

2.   Investing in Early Childhood Development

The expansion of social protection coverage increasingly reflects an appreciation by Pacific DMCs of the human development potential of comprehensive social protection systems. An important area of this expansion involves investments in early childhood development—a complex intersectoral initiative that includes social protection, health, education, water and sanitation, care practices, and child protection. Young children in the Pacific face high rates of malnutrition, particularly stunting.[193] With the high cost of nutritious food there, many families rely on high-calorie, nutrient-poor diets.[194] The pattern of under-five stunting rates reflects the need for key investments in early childhood nutrition in several Pacific DMCs (Figure 24).

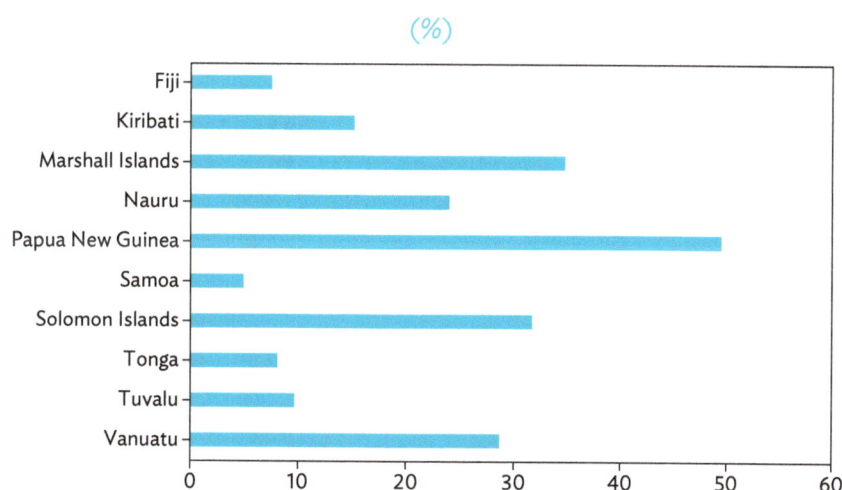

Figure 24: Stunting Rates of Children under Age 5 Years in the Pacific

(%)

Source: United Nations Children's Fund (UNICEF). Early Childhood Development. https://www.unicef.org/early-childhood-development (accessed 12 May 2022).

---

191   See Chapter IV for further details.
192   Key informant interviews with experts. For more information about the use of the WGQs, see SPC. Pacific Data Hub. https://pacificdata.org/.
193   UNICEF. 2018. UN Agencies Raise Alarm over Weakened Fight against Hunger and Malnutrition in Asia and the Pacific. Press release. 2 November. https://www.unicef.org/eap/press-releases/un-agencies-raise-alarm-over-weakened-fight-against-hunger-and-malnutrition-asia-and
194   M. Chung. 2010. Weaving Social Safety Nets in the Pacific. *Pacific Studies Series*. Manila: ADB.

The demographics of Pacific DMCs—with falling birth rates, rising life expectancy, and high rates of emigration—intensify the challenge of rising dependency ratios, which increasingly require higher growth rates of labor productivity to lift living standards. Recognizing this, governments across the region will benefit from child-sensitive social protection investments, particularly focusing on early childhood development. These investments have been identified as among the highest-yielding initiatives supporting future economic growth and prosperity.[195] These investments build cognitive capital that align economic growth and development strategies with economic opportunities.[196]

Regionally, the landmark 2017 Pasifika Call to Action on Early Childhood Development positioned child-sensitive social protection within a comprehensive early childhood development framework as the foundation for inclusive prosperity for the region.[197] Indeed, several Pacific island countries have already made child-sensitive social protection a priority. Nauru introduced a birth benefit in 2005 to help mothers cover the costs associated with a birth, providing A$300 to employed mothers and A$600 to unemployed mothers.[198] Niue started a one-time unconditional cash transfer in 2015 paid to the mother to support the needs of an infant. It also has had a nationwide child allowance program since 1995, which is a conditional cash transfer paid to the mother to support the education and welfare of children up to age 18 years.[199] The Government of the Cook Islands pays a cash benefit to caregivers of children up to age 12 years as well.[200]

This focus on children is likely to continue for two reasons. First, the Pacific region's demographic challenge of escalating dependency ratios has put rising living standards at risk unless labor productivity rates can increase faster than the population ages. Child-sensitive social protection investments improve child development and long-term health outcomes, building the human and cognitive capital foundations for sustainable improvements in labor productivity that drive future growth and prosperity. Second, as Pacific DMCs respond to the devastating human capital shock created by the COVID-19 crisis, comprehensive child-sensitive social protection investments in early childhood development most effectively tackle the medium- to long-term social and economic consequences of the crisis, taking maximum advantage of the changes in both work norms and remote collaboration technologies. These trends will improve the economic competitiveness

[195] J. Hoddinott et al. 2013. The Economic Rationale for Investing in Stunting Reduction. *Maternal and Child Nutrition*. 9 (Suppl 2). pp. 69–82.

[196] M. Samson, G. Fajth, and D. Francois. 2016. Cognitive Capital, Equity and Child Sensitive Social Protection in Asia and the Pacific. *BMJ Global Health*. 1 (Supp 2).

[197] Pacific Islands Forum. 2020. Information Paper No. 9: Early Childhood Development. https://www.forumsec.org/wp-content/uploads/2020/08/PIFS20FEMM.Info_.9-Early-Childhood-Development_Final.pdf.

[198] EPRI. 2021. Situational Analysis Report: Strengthening Social Protection in the Pacific–Nauru Social Protection Strategy Project. Cape Town.

[199] International Policy Centre for Inclusive Growth and UNICEF. 2019. *Social Protection in Asia and the Pacific: Inventory of Non-Contributory Programmes*. Brasília. https://www.unicef.org/pacificislands/media/706/file/Social-Protection-in-Asia-and-the-Pacific.pdf.

[200] Government of the Cook Islands, Ministry of Internal Affairs. 2014. Child Benefit Fact Sheet. https://www.intaff.gov.ck/?attachment_id=408#:~:text=The%20Child%20Benefit%20is%20paid,of%20their%20Cook%20Islands%20connections.

of Pacific DMCs in knowledge industries over the long term, as long as governments can support the skill sets of the labor force required to realize these opportunities.

In response to the global COVID-19 pandemic, regional stakeholders in the Pacific have highlighted the potential of digital technologies to open new green industries in the region and to offer new avenues for economic growth. For example, Samoa's long-term development strategy relies on innovating opportunities with knowledge-based technologies, which both are more environmentally sustainable and address the competitiveness challenges of a remote small island developing state, since digital products travel over the internet as easily from Apia as from Singapore.[201] Building this knowledge economy requires enhancing the skills of the labor force, strengthening the productive cognitive capital foundation through comprehensive child-sensitive social protection investments in early childhood. The Pacific Forum of Economic Ministers Meeting and Forum of Education Ministers have actively engaged in strengthening regional early childhood development initiatives to support these developmental impacts as well.[202]

3. Expanding Promotive Social Protection with a Focus on Youth

A life-cycle approach to social protection also includes a focus on youth development. Pacific DMCs will benefit from social protection initiatives that strengthen livelihoods and employment. Youth represent the main beneficiaries from such directions, since they face highest unemployment rates. Social protection works to enhance youth opportunities—starting with investments in cognitive capital in early childhood, continuing with programs that complement educational achievement, and leading to specific initiatives that support a transition to more productive livelihoods.

Fiji's national development plan emphasizes "empower[ing] Fijians so that they may graduate out of poverty."[203] It indicates that social protection should support education, pregnant women in rural areas, and other initiatives that build the long-term capabilities of the labor force. This includes expanding numbers for youth development programs, including empowerment and training initiatives with a focus on entrepreneurship, leadership, and tackling challenges associated with climate change (footnote 203).

On International Youth Day 2021, the Government of Tonga launched its first national youth policy, which integrated social protection instruments with initiatives supporting the health, employment, and well-being of youth.[204] Similarly, Kiribati's national youth policy integrates promotive elements, including education and skills

---

[201] Government of Samoa, Ministry of Finance. 2021. *Samoa 2040: Transforming Samoa to a Higher Growth Path*. Apia.

[202] UNICEF. 2021. *Country Office Annual Report 2021 Pacific Islands*. Suva. p. 6. ; and N. Tirivayi et al. 2020. A Rapid Review of Economic Policy and Social Protection Responses to Health and Economic Crises and Their Effects on Children: Lessons for the COVID-19 Pandemic Response. *Innocenti Working Papers*. New York: UNICEF.

[203] Government of Fiji. 2017. *Twenty-Year Development Plan 2017–2036*. https://www.adb.org/sites/default/files/linked-documents/LD4%205yr%20and%2020yr%20DP%20Transforming%20Fiji.pdf.

[204] SPC. 2021. National Policy Launch Heralds New Era for Tongan Youth. Web Stories. 17 August. https://www.spc.int/updates/blog/2021/08/national-policy-launch-heralds-new-era-for-tongan-youth.

building, economic participation, health and safety, social cohesion, and civic participation with a social protection lens, stating that "young people's assets, potential, capacity, and capability must be maximized so that they can respond effectively and efficiently to life's challenges without compromising the ability of future generations to meet their own needs."[205] Box 24 discusses an innovative approach to train young people to provide care support to older people in Tonga. The Solomon Islands national youth policy identifies six priority outcomes for its youth population: educational empowerment, economic empowerment, sustainable development, health, social inclusion, and access to information.[206]

Box 24: Building Intersectoral Synergies—Youth Technical and Vocational Education and Training for Aged Care in Tonga

The Government of Tonga and ADB are designing an integrated care system for older persons in Tonga. Supporting the National Aged Care Plan, the project will deliver integrated health and social care services and programs through community-based aged care centers. It will include preventive measures to promote healthy aging and reduce avoidable hospitalizations for older persons through various well-being approaches. The services will train and support caregivers—primarily youth—to not only enhance positive care experiences for their families but also to provide marketable skills to facilitate a pathway to formal employment in the social care sector. The integrated approach achieves comprehensive health, social care, and livelihood outcomes, strengthening the protective, preventive, and promotive pillars of a transformative social protection approach.

Source: ADB. 2021. *Initial Poverty and Social Analysis for Tonga: Integrated Aged Care Project.* Manila.

A regional initiative supports these national efforts for youth empowerment. The Pacific Youth Development Framework, 2014–2023, developed by the Secretariat of the Pacific Community, employs social protection approaches within a human rights framework to improve young people's access to various services and opportunities.[207] Moreover, the United Nations Economic and Social Commission for Asia and the Pacific (UNESCAP) maps out the overarching intergenerational social contract. Life-cycle social protection investments—including early childhood investments that build cognitive capital and youth initiatives that generate decent jobs—enable preferably green employment that supports economic growth and generates tax revenues that sustain benefit systems for the entire population, maximizing the Pacific's realization of demographic dividends.[208]

[205] Government of Kiribati, Ministry of Internal and Social Affairs. 2011. *Kiribati National Youth Policy, 2011–2015.* Tarawa. https://www.dropbox.com/s/wuvdrajajixijmc/KiribatiNationalYouthPolicy.pdf?dl=0.

[206] Government of Solomon Islands, Ministry of Women, Youth, Children and Family Affairs. 2017. *Solomon Islands National Youth Policy, 2017–2030.* Honiara. http://www.mwycfa.gov.sb/resources-2/strategic-plans-policies/youth-development-empowerment/6-solomon-islands-national-youth-policy-2017-2030/file.html.

[207] M. Carling. 2015. Strengthening Universality for Youth-Centred Development: The Pacific Approach. 12 August. https://socialprotection-humanrights.org/expertcom/strengthening-universality-for-youth-centred-development-the-pacific-approach.

[208] UNESCAP. n.d. Social Development: Youth Empowerment. Retrieved from https://www.unescap.org/our-work/social-development/youth-empowerment.

4.   Recognizing the Vital Role of Inclusive Digital Technologies

Strengthening the promotive and developmental focus on social protection's opportunities for youth employment, Pacific DMCs are recognizing the potential for inclusive digital technologies, not only to improve social protection delivery systems but also to expand livelihood opportunities for the region. Similarly, investing in childhood skills development increases the potential for inclusive digital technologies to contribute to development. Governments across the region are integrating these opportunities into their social protection systems and their larger development frameworks.

For example, Samoa 2040 recognizes that "digital technologies can act to stimulate business opportunities in e-commerce and e-services, as well as increas[e] productivity and growth in more traditional sectors such as agriculture and tourism."[209] The vision identifies that "the government needs to . . . boost education, skills, and digital literacy" outcomes that a comprehensive social protection system can support (footnote 209).

Similarly, Fiji's national development plan highlights inclusive digital infrastructure, digital banking, and digitalization in climate response and governance. Indeed, Fiji has been providing exemplary digital responses to the COVID-19 pandemic; the government and Fiji National Provident Fund employ digital payment mechanisms to deliver COVID-19 assistance, providing options for the mobile phone money transfer service through Vodafone, Inkk, Digicel, or Post Fiji.[210] While the government paid the initial emergency COVID-19 cash transfers to street vendors and other affected workers directly through their bank accounts, it provides subsequent benefits through a mobile money platform, finding that this significantly lowers delivery costs.[211] Such mobile technology also supports social distancing and other public health measures, including contact tracing, and the Ministry of Communications negotiated with Vodafone and Digicel for free data allocations.

The application of digital technologies to social protection remains in its early stages in the Pacific, however. A recent World Bank report indicated that "the global COVID-19 pandemic has further underscored the importance of accelerating digital development, particularly in the Pacific Islands region....[which] has been particularly isolated by travel restrictions and severe disruptions across all economic sectors."[212] Box 25 discusses the implications of digital technology gaps in Tuvalu. The issues described in this report remain highly relevant, particularly in regard to the urgency of improving digital infrastructure, enabling digital payments, boosting digital skills, and enacting legislation to protect digital transactions and to safeguard privacy. Box 25 describes the experience of Tuvalu in recognizing the importance of reliable digital infrastructure.

---

[209]   Government of Samoa, Ministry of Finance. 2021. *Samoa 2040: Transforming Samoa to a Higher Growth Path.* Apia.

[210]   I. Danford. 2020. Total of $13.95M paid out so far by FNPF and the government through the COVID-19 withdrawal assistance. *Fiji Village.* 21 April. https://www.fijivillage.com/news/Total-of-1395M-paid-out-so-far-by-FNPF-and-the-government-through-the-COVID-19-withdrawal-assistance-rx854f/

[211]   UNDP and UN Women. 2021. COVID-19 Global Gender Response Tracker. Version 2. https://data.undp.org/gendertracker/ (accessed on 12 May 2022).

[212]   World Bank. 2020. *Accelerating Practical Digital Development in the Solomon Islands.* Washington, DC. https://openknowledge.worldbank.org/handle/10986/35319.

Box 25: Digital Technology Gaps and Learning in Tuvalu

The closure of schools in Tuvalu in response to the COVID-19 pandemic disrupted learning, particularly since authorities were not prepared to provide alternative means of distance education. Even when schools reopened, several parents and guardians refused to allow their children to return due to health concerns. In addition, some families worried that logistical constraints facing interisland ferries would prevent students from returning home immediately if a further outbreak occurred in the country.

The government thus has recognized the value of e-learning as a viable alternative to physical learning. However, the cost of data connectivity and unreliability of internet connections in Tuvalu create significant barriers. Investments in information and communication infrastructure and initiatives to ensure access to inclusive digital technologies can improve the quality of education in normal times as well as strengthen resilience to disruptive shocks.

Source: ADB. 2020. *Pacific Economic Monitor.* December. Manila.

The requirement of social distancing during the pandemic has accelerated the adoption of digital technologies (i.e., registration, payments, and monitoring systems). The pandemic has aligned a number of key driving forces, including urgency, scale, and public health concerns, all of which have propelled the case for digital registration systems. Manual paper-based systems are slow to implement, particularly when they must reach thousands of people. In addition, the in-person nature of face-to-face registration systems compounds public health risks during a pandemic caused by an airborne virus. Digital registration systems tackle these concerns—enabling rapid expansion to thousands of people in a safe manner.

While governments around the world have invested in improving digital social protection systems to build resilience, Pacific DMCs have also begun to leverage inclusive technologies to improve social insurance and social assistance programs. For example, the Vanuatu National Provident Fund has partnered with the International Labour Organization and the United Nations Capital Development Fund, worked with Vodafone, to launch M-Vatu, a payment gateway that enables informal sector workers, including the self-employed, to access social security services through their mobile phones. The International Labour Organization has planned similar initiatives in Fiji and Tonga.[213] The Pacific region relies heavily on provident funds as contributory mechanisms, which are more administratively intensive compared with noncontributory cash transfer programs. A focus on inclusive digital technologies can provide the necessary access to ensure that mobile payment gateways can support expansions of these mechanisms to the most vulnerable.

Ensuring digital equity represents one example requiring intersectoral collaboration and an ambitious initiative on an unprecedented scale. The COVID-19 crisis has demonstrated the extraordinary value of internet access in strengthening resilience

213   ILO. 2021. Innovation to Increase Access to Social Security in Vanuatu. ILO in the Pacific. 31 August. https://www.ilo.org/suva/public-information/WCMS_818273/lang--en/index.htm.

in every domain: digital technologies support telemedicine and mental health support; internet-based educational technologies improve the quality of remote learning strategies; and apps provide effective substitutes for markets closed by the pandemic.

Yet the COVID-19 pandemic has also elevated the challenge of digital equity to a complex problem. The most vulnerable people often have the least access to digital technologies, creating a double shock when governments tackle crises with technology-focused responses. Technology ministries are typically inappropriately structured to tackle equity objectives. The technology-affected spheres of public policy have multiplied during the pandemic to include health, education, commerce, justice, transport, food security, and social protection. Thus, the challenge of ensuring digital equity will require unprecedented cooperation and collaboration across government ministries, departments, and agencies as well as with international development partners. Ensuring digital equity represents one example requiring intersectoral collaboration and an ambitious initiative on a never-before-seen scale.

The global pandemic presents an opportunity to change the pattern of social returns to alternative public investments. For example, early childhood development initiatives offer the potential to offset the catastrophic long-term costs of the pandemic's human capital shock. These patterns, trends, and opportunities can interact to strengthen the knowledge-based economic sectors, aligning the priorities of crisis response and recovery with the major economic growth opportunities of the 21st century.

Discussions with experts have corroborated the extent to which development partners are supporting digital technologies across the Pacific—for management information systems, registration, and payment platforms, often with a strong focus on financial inclusion. Reluctance to trust mobile wallets and limited network coverage dampen the developmental potential of the technologies, however. Steady telecommunications investments can expand the reach of these opportunities. PNG's new nutrition-sensitive social protection program, funded by the Government of Australia and the World Bank, is planning to employ mobile money payment platforms, with Digicel providing participants with phones and connectivity.

Note that any future digital intervention wields a double-edged sword. Positive benefits come directly through improved remote learning, better telehealth services, proactive social protection delivery, strengthened e-markets, more adaptive livelihoods, richer information access, and enhanced financial inclusion. They also come indirectly by further fueling forces to expand digital inclusion and creating greater incentives for excluded households to overcome barriers to access. On the other hand, there is a risk of persistent digital divide unless these initiatives explicitly address equity, particularly by ensuring universal access to connectivity and associated technologies, including hardware. All people must also benefit from the necessary consumer protection and regulations to guarantee that unscrupulous operators do not use digital (and financial) inclusion to adversely impact the vulnerable by subjecting them to various violations of privacy and fraudulent and unfair financial practices.

5. Developing National Social Protection Strategies

In 2009, a regional review of social protection found that no Pacific DMC had developed or implemented a national social protection policy or strategy that tackled deprivation and vulnerability.[214] Many countries have resisted conventional notions of poverty, recognizing instead that some households faced "hardship."[215] The COVID-19 pandemic—both with its devastating economic impacts as well as its foreshadowing of future crises—is accelerating governments' embrace of formal plans that document social protection commitments and approaches. The success of social protection responses to the pandemic has demonstrated to governments and their development partners its potential in not only strengthening shock-responsive systems but also reinforcing the social dimension of the new mix of climate, development, and equity strategies that will be required for a transition to a green and sustainable society.

Global and regional development partners are providing resources and expertise that support this initiative. ADB is supporting the development of national social protection policies or strategies in PNG, Nauru, and other DMCs in the region. The United Nation's Joint SDG Fund is providing technical assistance to the Cook Islands, Niue, Samoa, and other Pacific DMCs, including support to develop national social protection policy frameworks. This assistance builds on momentum for national policies in several other countries.

Samoa conducted consultations in 2021 to move forward with a national social protection policy that aims "to prevent and reduce national and life-cycle poverty, vulnerability, and inequality prevalence and risks" with a goal "to establish a gender-sensitive and age-appropriate social protection framework to ensure a minimum social protection floor for all Samoan citizens for a life of dignity."[216] While recognizing the importance of global best practices, the policy process emphasizes "promoting the strengths of local institutions, principles and values" (footnote 216). Other policies similarly focus on the synergy between formal and traditional systems.

6. Integrating Comprehensive Social Protection Programming That Strengthens Development

The trend toward formalizing national social protection policies and strategies enables and reinforces another vital direction: the increasing integration of more comprehensive social protection programming. While not all Pacific DMCs are planning to develop separate national social protection frameworks, some have incorporated key elements of more comprehensive strategies into their national development plans and visions. For example, Fiji does not have a national social protection policy but the national development plan substantially addresses social assistance schemes, affordable housing, gender equality, the inclusion of persons

---

[214]   AusAID. 2009. Social Protection in the Pacific: Scoping Report. Unpublished.
[215]   C. Costella and O. Ivaschenko. 2015. Integrating Disaster Response and Climate Resilience in Social Protection Programs in the Pacific Island Countries. *Social Protection and Labor Discussion Papers.* No. 1507. Washington, DC: World Bank.
[216]   L. Lesa. 2021. Exploring Social Protection Options in Samoa. UNDP Samoa. 30 June. https://undpsamoa.medium.com/exploring-social-protection-options-in-samoa-855f1aef4c96.

with disabilities, and climate change. Discussions with experts have highlighted the importance of robust data to support complex social protection programming. To strengthen this, the Pacific Statistics Methods Board is assessing the incorporation of modules into the region's main household income and expenditure survey (HIES) to gather data on the impact of climate change on livelihoods and social welfare.[217]

The Pacific region's cohesive collaborative approaches strengthen opportunities for policy diffusion and increase the likelihood that the trend toward national social protection policies and strategies will endure. The Pacific Island Forum's initiative of a regional council for early childhood development strategies provides a model for cooperation and directly reinforces key elements that support integrated policy development. This trend of consolidating national social protection strategies reinforces the first three trends. Comprehensive social protection policies and frameworks support delivery of integrated life-cycle approaches, reaching all vulnerable groups while better enabling complex outcomes, including nutrition and early childhood development investments as well as promotive opportunities for youth and older working-age adults. Discussions with experts have highlighted the importance of government ownership in ensuring the success of these policy mechanisms.

7.   Optimizing the Mix of Climate, Development, and Equity Goals

Integrated and comprehensive social protection systems offer potential for tackling challenges posed by climate change. In addition, policy makers increasingly recognize that social protection offers a flexible instrument that better enables successful climate change mitigation and adaptation strategies. As disasters triggered by natural hazards become more frequent and severe—and the most vulnerable groups often bear a disproportionate share of the cost—Pacific DMCs need to gradually integrate social protection responses into comprehensive systems for disaster risk management and climate change adaptation.

The Pacific region leads the world in terms of commitment to tackling climate change. For example, Fiji was the first country to ratify the Paris Climate Accords.[218] While Vanuatu's National Policy on Climate Change and Disaster-Induced Displacement does not employ the term "social protection," the adopted instruments include the social protection sector's core tools, including those that promote access to health and education services and that strengthen livelihoods protection.[219]

[217]   SPC. 2021. 8th Pacific Statistics Methods Board Meeting Summary Report and Outcomes. https://sdd.spc.int/digital_library/8th-pacific-statistics-methods-board-meeting-psmb-summary-report-and-outcomes.

[218]   World Bank. 2021. World Bank and Fiji Sign Agreement to Reduce Forest Emissions and Boost Climate Resilience. Press release. 28 January. https://www.worldbank.org/en/news/press-release/2021/01/28/world-bank-and-fiji-sign-agreement-to-reduce-forest-emissions-and-boost-climate-resilience#:~:text=%E2%80%9CFiji%20continues%20to%20demonstrate%20its,commitment%20to%20tackling%20climate%20change.

[219]   Government of Vanuatu. 2018. *National Policy on Climate Change and Disaster-Induced Displacement.* 28 January. https://www.iom.int/sites/g/files/tmzbdl486/files/press_release/file/iom-vanuatu-policy-climate-change-disaster-induced-displacement-2018.pdf.

Pacific DMCs are developing climate-smart rural development strategies that reinvent traditional agriculture practices that strengthen food security and reduce climate vulnerability, for example, by piloting salt- and drought-tolerant crops.[220] These innovations involve risks that comprehensive social protection systems can better manage, particularly with promotive instruments. Social protection's transformative function also plays a vital role—for example, in addressing gender-based land-right inequality, as climate change is reducing the availability of arable land in PNG and other Pacific DMCs (footnote 220). The Pacific region's commitment to tackling climate change will require a growing commitment to adaptive social protection to strengthen the synergy between climate and development strategies.

Governments and development partners can do more to integrate climate and development priorities into their development plans and strategies. Today, shock-responsive approaches influence every aspect of social protection systems, demonstrating the importance of anticipatory actions that ensure the necessary mechanisms are in place before crisis strikes. ADB's new regional strategy, Pacific Approach, 2021–2025, motivated in part by the increasing frequency and intensity of climate shocks, adopts a comprehensive approach that integrates social protection system support with initiatives to strengthen public and private sector responses to shocks.[221] The global COVID-19 crisis has tested national and global approaches and identified the shortcomings from greater shocks that climate change threatens. Pacific DMCs and their development partners will likely increasingly rely on social protection's potential to help optimize the mix of climate, development, and equity strategies.

Conclusion

Over the next few decades, Pacific DMCs stand to benefit from realizing the full potential of developing comprehensive and integrated social protection systems that will strengthen inclusive social development and equitable economic growth across the region. Even prior to the COVID-19 crisis, the sector had been expanding at a steady pace, and the pandemic's system of cascading and interacting shocks has demonstrated the universality of vulnerability and accelerated the adoption of social assistance, social insurance, and LMPs. The recent crisis has demonstrated the limits of Pacific traditional systems and reinforced the governments' commitments to reach vulnerable groups, particularly older persons and persons with disabilities. Importantly, Pacific DMCs have increasingly recognized social protection investments

---

[220] E. Mcleod et al. 2019. Lessons from the Pacific Islands—Adapting to Climate Change by Supporting Social and Ecological Resilience. *Frontiers in Marine Science*. 6. https://www.frontiersin.org/article/10.3389/fmars.2019.00289; and E. Mcleod et al. 2018. Raising the Voices of Pacific Island Women to Inform Climate Adaptation Policies. *Marine Policy*. 93. pp. 178–185. https://doi.org/https://doi.org/10.1016/j.marpol.2018.03.011.

[221] ADB. 2021. ADB Generally Endorses New Strategy for Pacific Small Island Developing States. News release. 30 June. https://www.adb.org/news/adb-generally-endorses-new-strategy-pacific-small-island-developing-states. The news release quotes ADB director general for the Pacific Leah Gutierrez, "This new and tailored approach to our work is also motivated by the growing frequency and intensity of climate change and natural hazards in the region."

in early childhood development, building the foundation for human and cognitive capital that drives future prosperity. Similarly, social protection initiatives have focused on harnessing the demographic dividend by promoting youth development and opportunities.

These life-cycle investments strengthen social protection's promotive and transformative potential, enabling households to build human capital, manage livelihood risks, invest in more sustainable livelihoods, and strengthen their resilience to future shocks by achieving a diversity of developmental outcomes. Increasingly, government investments in digital inclusion are reinforcing all of these directions, building a more shock-responsive and adaptive social protection system that strengthens linkages to telehealth services, remote education, e-markets, adaptive livelihoods, financial inclusion, systems-driven social protection, and other developmental areas. While these technological innovations offer substantial promise, they also pose significant risks that require governments to build consumer protection mechanisms and to ensure effective regulation against abuses.

These expanded commitments to social protection contribute to a larger system for managing risk that will better enable Pacific DMCs to optimize a mix of climate and development strategies. Pacific DMCs are increasingly formalizing their commitments with national social protection policies and strategies; these frameworks produce vital synergies, enabling climate and development policies to work better together in two ways. First, they enable people to better manage the entire life cycle of risks associated with the transitions that mitigating climate change will require. Second, they provide Pacific DMCs with flexible tools for improving the equity impacts of the sometimes painful and costly adjustments that sustainable development strategies may need. Social protection provides Pacific DMCs with the pro-poor comprehensive and integrated climate and development policy frameworks, promising to support a future of inclusive social development and equitable economic growth.

Appendix

Table A1: Social Protection Indicator by Category, 2018
(% of GDP per capita)

Country	Overall SPI	Social Insurance	Social Assistance	Labor Market Programs
High Income	**6.1**	**2.7**	**3.4**	**0.0**
Cook Islands	3.3	0.5	2.8	...
Nauru	2.9	0.1	2.8	...
Niue	7.8	1.1	6.7	...
Palau	10.4	9.2	1.1	0.1
Upper Middle Income	**6.2**	**3.9**	**2.0**	**0.2**
Fiji	3.3	2.2	1.1	0.0
Marshall Islands	10.3	8.3	0.9	1.1
FSM	5.0	4.2	0.8	...
Tonga	1.5	1.0	0.4	0.1
Tuvalu	10.7	3.7	7.0	...
Lower Middle Income	**4.4**	**2.2**	**0.9**	**1.3**
Kiribati	11.1	3.7	0.9	6.5
Papua New Guinea	0.9	0.9	...	0.0
Samoa	3.4	2.4	0.9	0.1
Solomon Islands	3.0	2.9	0.0	0.1
Vanuatu	3.4	0.9	2.5	0.0
Unweighted Pacific Average	**5.5**	**2.9**	**2.0**	**0.6**

... = no data, 0.0 = value is less than 0.01, FSM = Federated States of Micronesia, GDP = gross domestic product, SPI = Social Protection Indicator.

Source: ADB estimates based on consultants' country reports.

Table A2: **Social Protection Indicator by Depth, Breadth, and Category, 2018**

	Depth of Social Protection Benefits (% of GDP per capita)				Breadth of Social Protection Coverage (% of target beneficiaries)			
	Overall Depth	Social Insurance	Social Assistance	LMPs	Overall Breadth	Social Insurance	Social Assistance	LMPs
High Income	**10.3**	**23.4**	**9.7**	**0.8**	**59.6**	**26.9**	**32.3**	**0.4**
Cook Islands	8.9	33.0	8.0	...	36.6	1.4	35.2	...
Nauru	7.9	41.3	7.6	...	36.9	0.3	36.6	...
Niue	15.1	9.5	16.7	...	51.6	11.7	39.8	...
Palau	9.2	9.8	6.3	3.3	113.3	94.3	17.5	1.5
Upper Middle Income	**29.8**	**126.9**	**18.2**	**3.2**	**30.1**	**4.4**	**17.9**	**7.8**
Fiji	8.5	29.0	3.4	7.2	39.4	7.7	30.9	0.8
Marshall Islands	17.7	108.7	3.7	4.2	58.0	7.6	24.2	26.2
Tonga	16.9	136.1	10.0	1.4	8.6	0.7	3.9	4.0
Tuvalu	75.9	233.7	55.7	...	14.2	1.6	12.6	...
Lower Middle Income	**65.8**	**141.7**	**14.8**	**38.3**	**14.9**	**2.2**	**11.1**	**1.5**
FSM	81.6	89.6	54.5	...	6.1	4.7	1.4	...
Kiribati	118.1	180.4	22.6	189.3	9.4	2.1	3.9	3.4
Papua New Guinea	71.4	86.6	...	4.0	1.3	1.0	...	0.3
Samoa	15.7	62.5	5.8	2.5	21.8	3.9	16.2	1.7
Solomon Islands	100.5	242.1	0.2	32.8	3.0	1.2	1.6	0.2
Vanuatu	7.2	189.2	5.7	0.9	47.6	0.5	43.7	3.5
Unweighted Pacific Average	**39.6**	**103.7**	**14.3**	**17.5**	**32.0**	**9.9**	**19.1**	**3.0**

... = no data, FSM = Federated States of Micronesia, GDP = gross domestic product, LMP = labor market program, SPI = Social Protection Indicator.

Source: ADB estimates based on consultants' country reports.

Table A3: Progress on Social Protection Indicator by Category, 2009–2018

(% of GDP per capita)

Country	2009				2012				2015				2018			
	SPI	SI	SA	LMP	SPI	SI	SA	LMP	SPI	SI	SA	LMP	SPI	SI	SA	LMP
Cook Islands	...	...	...	...	3.0	0.3	2.7	...	2.5	0.2	2.3	...	3.3	0.5	2.8	...
Fiji	6.2	5.6	0.6	0.0	4.5	3.9	0.6	...	3.3	2.8	0.5	0.0	3.3	2.2	1.1	0.0
FSM	...	...	...	...	7.9	7.2	0.7	...	6.1	5.3	0.8	...	5.0	4.2	0.8	...
Kiribati	...	...	...	...	11.5	7.1	1.0	3.4	10.4	5.9	0.9	3.6	11.1	3.7	0.9	6.5
Nauru	0.9	0.3	0.6	...	0.7	0.1	0.6	...	4.3	0.1	4.2	...	2.9	0.1	2.8	...
Niue	...	...	...	...	...	...	...	...	...	...	...	...	7.8	1.1	6.7	...
Palau	7.7	6.7	1.0	0.0	7.7	7.4	0.3	0.0	8.5	8.0	0.5	0.0	10.4	9.2	1.1	0.1
Papua New Guinea	0.6	0.6	...	0.0	0.8	0.8	...	0.0	0.7	0.7	...	0.0	0.9	0.9	...	0.0
Marshall Islands	4.7	3.0	1.2	0.5	7.7	6.4	0.8	0.5	10.6	9.0	0.8	0.8	10.3	8.3	0.9	1.1
Samoa	2.8	1.7	1.0	0.1	2.7	1.7	1.0	0.0	3.3	2.2	1.0	0.1	3.4	2.4	0.9	0.1
Solomon Islands	1.0	1.0	0.0	0.0	1.4	1.3	0.0	0.1	3.4	2.8	0.0	0.6	3.0	2.9	0.0	0.1
Tonga	...	...	...	...	0.7	0.5	0.2	...	1.8	1.3	0.4	0.1	1.5	1.0	0.4	0.1
Tuvalu	...	...	...	...	...	...	...	...	...	...	...	...	10.7	3.7	7.0	...
Vanuatu	0.6	0.4	0.2	0.0	0.8	0.8	0.0	0.0	1.3	1.2	0.1	0.0	3.4	0.9	2.5	0.0
Unweighted Pacific Average	**3.1**	**2.4**	**0.6**	**0.1**	**3.3**	**2.8**	**0.4**	**0.1**	**4.4**	**3.4**	**0.9**	**0.2**	**4.7**	**3.4**	**1.2**	**0.2**

... = no data, 0.0 = value is less than 0.01, FSM = Federated States of Micronesia, GDP = gross domestic product, LMP = labor market program, SA = social assistance, SI = social insurance, SPI = Social Protection Indicator.

Source: ADB estimates based on consultants' country reports.

Table A4: Progress in the Social Protection Indicator by Category and Income Group, 2009–2018
(% of GDP per capita)

Country	2009				2012				2015				2018			
	SPI	SI	SA	LMP	SPI	SI	SA	LMP	SPI	SI	SA	LMP	SPI	SI	SA	LMP
High Income	**4.3**	**3.5**	**0.8**	**0.0**	**4.2**	**3.8**	**0.5**	**0.0**	**6.4**	**4.1**	**2.4**	**0.0**	**6.7**	**4.7**	**2.0**	**0.1**
Cook Islands	..	..	..	..	3.0	0.3	2.7	..	2.5	0.2	2.3	..	3.3	0.5	2.8	..
Nauru	0.9	0.3	0.6	0.0	0.7	0.1	0.6	0.0	4.3	0.1	4.2	0.0	2.9	0.1	2.8	0.0
Niue	..	..	..	..	..	..	..	..	..	..	..	..	7.8	1.1	6.7	..
Palau	7.7	6.0	1.0	0.0	7.7	7.4	0.3	0.0	8.5	8.0	0.5	0.0	10.4	9.2	1.1	0.1
Upper Middle Income	**5.5**	**4.3**	**0.9**	**0.3**	**6.1**	**5.2**	**0.7**	**0.5**	**7.0**	**5.9**	**0.7**	**0.4**	**6.8**	**5.3**	**1.0**	**0.6**
Fiji	6.2	5.6	0.6	..	4.5	3.9	0.6	..	3.3	2.8	0.5	..	3.3	2.2	1.1	..
Marshall Islands	4.7	3.0	1.2	0.5	7.7	6.4	0.8	0.5	10.6	9.0	0.8	0.8	10.3	8.3	0.9	1.1
Tonga	..	..	..	..	0.7	0.5	0.2	0.0	1.8	1.3	0.4	0.1	1.5	1.0	0.4	0.1
Tuvalu	..	..	..	..	..	..	..	..	..	..	..	..	10.7	3.7	7.0	..
Lower Middle Income	**1.3**	**0.9**	**0.3**	**0.0**	**1.4**	**1.2**	**0.3**	**0.0**	**2.2**	**1.7**	**0.3**	**0.2**	**2.7**	**1.8**	**0.9**	**0.1**
FSM	..	..	..	..	7.9	7.2	0.7	..	6.1	5.3	0.8	..	5.0	4.2	0.8	..
Kiribati	..	..	..	..	11.5	7.1	1.0	3.4	10.4	5.9	0.9	3.6	11.1	3.7	0.9	6.5
Papua New Guinea	0.6	0.6	..	0.0	0.8	0.8	..	0.0	0.7	0.7	..	0.0	0.9	0.9	..	0.0
Samoa	2.8	1.7	1.0	0.1	2.7	1.7	1.0	0.1	3.3	2.2	1.0	0.1	3.4	2.4	0.9	0.1
Solomon Islands	1.0	1.0	0.0	0.0	1.4	1.3	0.0	0.1	3.4	2.8	0.0	0.6	3.0	2.9	0.0	0.1
Vanuatu	0.6	0.4	0.2	0.0	0.8	0.8	0.0	0.0	1.3	1.2	0.1	0.0	3.4	0.9	2.5	0.0
Unweighted Pacific Average	**3.1**	**2.4**	**0.6**	**0.1**	**3.3**	**2.8**	**0.4**	**0.1**	**4.4**	**3.4**	**0.9**	**0.2**	**4.7**	**3.4**	**1.2**	**0.2**

.. = no data, 0.0 = value is less than 0.01, FSM = Federated States of Micronesia, GDP = gross domestic product, LMP = labor market program, SA = social assistance, SI = social insurance, SPI= Social Protection Indicator.

Source: ADB estimates based on consultants' country reports.

Table A5: Progress in Depth of Benefits by Country, 2009–2018
(% of GDP per capita)

Country	2009				2012				2015				2018			
	Depth	SI	SA	LMP	Depth	SI	SA	LMP	Depth	SI	SA	LMP	Depth	SI	SA	LMP
Cook Islands	...	...	...	...	8.6	30.6	8.1	...	7.2	18.2	6.8	...	8.9	33.0	8.0	...
Fiji	53.8	77.5	16.1	3.4	30.0	70.2	6.3	4.9	12.1	42.4	2.4	8.1	8.5	29.0	3.4	7.2
FSM	...	...	...	...	86.0	109.2	27.4	...	86.2	98.2	48.9	...	81.6	89.6	54.5	...
Kiribati	117.3	...	...	...	117.3	189.8	31.6	115.2	99.3	134.1	28.2	128.3	118.1	180.4	22.6	189.3
Nauru	14.8	31.8	11.9	0.0	11.0	19.4	9.9	...	11.7	31.6	11.6	...	7.9	41.3	7.6	...
Niue	...	...	...	...	...	...	...	...	...	...	...	...	15.1	9.5	16.7	...
Palau	25.7	37.6	8.0	0.8	7.2	7.9	2.1	9.0	8.8	9.4	4.3	6.2	9.2	9.8	6.3	3.3
Papua New Guinea	516.1	519.9	0.0	72.0	503.5	544.5	...	64.4	189.2	329.3	...	14.8	71.4	86.6	...	4.0
Marshall Islands	17.6	54.5	19.5	3.8	36.0	111.0	26.4	3.8	47.2	123.7	62.3	5.8	17.7	108.7	3.7	4.2
Samoa	7.0	90.7	2.8	3.4	5.9	83.2	2.3	3.7	7.1	97.9	2.3	4.1	15.7	62.5	5.8	2.5
Solomon Islands	68.0	104.9	43.5	4.5	53.6	243.7	2.6	6.4	124.1	272.4	3.3	48.5	100.5	242.1	0.2	32.8
Tonga	...	...	...	...	17.6	312.0	10.2	0.7	22.8	235.8	9.5	1.6	16.9	136.1	10.0	1.4
Tuvalu	...	...	...	...	...	...	...	...	...	...	...	...	75.9	233.7	55.7	...
Vanuatu	15.3	95.2	7.1	16.8	4.8	250.7	0.3	3.1	4.9	218.4	0.4	1.9	7.2	189.2	5.7	0.9
Unweighted Pacific Average	**89.8**	**126.5**	**13.6**	**13.1**	**81.6**	**166.3**	**6.2**	**11.9**	**50.6**	**140.6**	**10.8**	**11.2**	**29.8**	**96.2**	**4.1**	**6.9**

... = no data, FSM = Federated States of Micronesia, GDP = gross domestic product, LMP = labor market program, SA = social assistance, SI = social insurance, SPI = Social Protection Indicator.

Source: ADB estimates based on consultants' country reports.

Table A6: Progress in Depth of Benefits, 2009–2018
(% of GDP per capita)

Country	2009				2012				2015				2018			
	SPI	SI	SA	LMP	SPI	SI	SA	LMP	SPI	SI	SA	LMP	SPI	SI	SA	LMP
High Income	**20.3**	**34.7**	**10.1**	**0.4**	**9.1**	**13.7**	**6.0**	**4.5**	**10.3**	**20.5**	**8.0**	**3.1**	**8.6**	**25.6**	**7.0**	**3.3**
Cook Islands	...	...	...	...	8.6	30.6	8.1	...	7.2	18.2	6.8	...	8.9	33.0	8.0	...
Nauru	14.8	31.8	11.9	...	11.0	19.4	9.9	...	11.7	31.6	11.6	...	7.9	41.3	7.6	...
Niue	...	...	...	...	86.0	109.2	27.4	0.0	86.2	98.2	48.9	0.0	15.1	9.5	16.7	...
Palau	25.7	37.6	8.2	0.8	7.2	7.9	2.1	9.0	8.8	9.4	4.3	6.2	9.2	9.8	6.3	3.3
Upper Middle Income	**35.7**	**66.0**	**17.8**	**3.6**	**33.3**	**90.6**	**16.4**	**4.4**	**29.7**	**83.1**	**32.4**	**7.0**	**13.1**	**68.9**	**3.6**	**5.7**
Fiji	53.8	77.5	16.1	3.4	30.6	70.2	6.3	4.9	12.1	42.4	2.4	8.1	8.5	29.0	3.4	7.2
Marshall Islands	17.6	54.5	19.5	3.8	36.0	111.0	26.4	3.8	47.2	123.7	62.3	5.8	17.7	108.7	3.7	4.2
Tonga	...	...	...		17.6	312.0	10.2	0.7	22.8	235.8	9.5	1.6	16.9	136.1	10.0	1.4
Tuvalu	...	...	...	...	...	...	...	...	...	...	...	...	75.9	233.7	55.7	...
Lower Middle Income	**151.6**	**202.7**	**13.4**	**24.2**	**142.0**	**280.5**	**1.3**	**19.4**	**81.3**	**229.5**	**2.0**	**17.3**	**48.7**	**145.1**	**3.9**	**10.1**
FSM	...	...	...	...	86.0	109.2	27.4	...	86.2	98.2	48.9	...	81.6	89.6	54.5	...
Kiribati	...	...	...	...	117.3	189.8	31.6	115.2	99.3	134.1	28.2	128.3	118.1	180.4	22.6	189.3
Papua New Guinea	516.1	519.9	...	72.0	503.5	544.5	...	64.4	189.2	329.3	...	14.8	71.4	86.6	...	4.0
Samoa	7.0	90.7	2.8	3.4	5.9	83.2	2.3	3.7	7.1	97.9	2.3	4.1	15.7	62.5	5.8	2.5
Solomon Islands	68.0	104.9	43.5	4.5	53.6	243.7	2.6	6.4	124.1	272.4	3.3	48.5	100.5	242.1	0.2	32.8
Vanuatu	15.3	95.2	7.1	16.8	4.8	250.7	0.3	3.1	4.9	218.4	0.4	1.9	7.2	189.2	5.7	0.9
Unweighted Pacific Average	**89.8**	**126.5**	**13.6**	**13.1**	**81.6**	**166.3**	**6.2**	**11.9**	**50.6**	**140.6**	**12.4**	**11.2**	**29.8**	**96.2**	**4.7**	**7.8**

... = no data, 0.0 = value is less than 0.01, FSM = Federated States of Micronesia, GDP = gross domestic product, LMP = labor market program, SA = social assistance, SI = social insurance, SPI = Social Protection Indicator.

Source: ADB estimates based on consultants' country reports.

Table A7: Progress in Breadth of Coverage, 2009–2018
(% of total target beneficiaries)

	2009				2012				2015				2018			
	Overall	SI	SA	LMP	Overall	SI	SA	LMP	Overall	SI	SA	LMP	Overall	SI	SA	LMP
Cook Islands	...	...	...	...	34.5	0.7	33.8	...	34.6	1.1	33.5	...	36.6	1.4	35.2	...
Fiji	11.5	7.1	4.0	0.4	14.6	5.6	8.7	0.4	27.3	6.6	20.5	0.3	39.4	7.7	30.9	0.8
FSM	...	...	...	...	9.2	6.6	2.6	...	7.1	5.3	1.7	...	6.1	4.7	1.4	...
Kiribati	...	...	...	...	9.8	3.8	3.1	2.9	10.5	4.4	3.3	2.8	9.4	2.1	3.9	3.4
Nauru	5.8	0.8	5.0	...	6.7	0.7	6.0	...	37.1	0.3	36.9	...	36.9	0.3	36.6	...
Niue	...	...	...	...	...	...	...	...	...	...	...	0.0	51.6	11.7	39.8	...
Palau	29.9	17.9	11.8	0.2	108.0	94.2	13.7	0.1	97.3	84.6	12.6	0.1	113.3	94.3	17.5	1.5
Papua New Guinea	0.1	0.1	...	0.0	0.2	0.1	...	0.0	0.4	0.2	...	0.2	1.3	1.0	...	0.3
Marshall Islands	26.9	5.4	6.1	15.4	21.3	5.8	3.0	12.6	22.5	7.3	1.3	13.9	58.0	7.6	24.2	26.2
Samoa	39.6	1.9	37.1	0.6	45.4	2.0	42.5	0.9	45.9	2.3	42.6	1.0	21.8	3.9	16.2	1.7
Solomon Islands	1.4	0.9	0.0	0.5	2.7	0.5	0.0	2.1	2.8	1.0	0.5	1.2	3.0	1.2	1.6	0.2
Tonga	...	...	...	...	4.2	0.2	1.8	2.2	7.7	0.6	4.0	3.2	8.6	0.7	3.9	4.0
Tuvalu	...	...	...	...	...	...	...	...	...	...	...	...	14.2	1.6	12.6	...
Vanuatu	4.0	0.4	3.6	0.0	17.6	0.3	16.2	1.1	26.6	0.5	24.2	2.0	47.6	0.5	43.7	3.5
Unweighted Pacific Average	14.9	4.3	8.5	2.1	27.1	13.7	11.3	2.2	32.5	12.9	17.3	2.3	40.2	14.6	21.3	4.3

... = no data, FSM = Federated States of Micronesia, LMP = labor market program, SA = social assistance, SI = social insurance, SPI = Social Protection Indicator.

Source: ADB estimates based on consultants' country reports.

Table A8: Progress in Breadth of Coverage, 2009–2018
(% of total target beneficiaries)

	2009				2012				2015				2018			
	Overall	SI	SA	LMP	Overall	SI	SA	LMP	Overall	SI	SA	LMP	Overall	SI	SA	LMP
High Income	**17.9**	**9.4**	**8.4**	**0.2**	**57.4**	**47.5**	**9.9**	**0.1**	**67.2**	**42.5**	**24.8**	**0.1**	**75.1**	**47.3**	**27.1**	**1.5**
Cook Islands	...	...	...	...	34.5	0.7	33.8	...	34.6	1.1	33.5	...	36.6	1.4	35.2	...
Nauru	5.8	0.8	5.0	...	6.7	0.7	6.0	...	37.1	0.3	36.9	...	36.9	0.3	36.6	...
Niue	...	...	...	...	...	...	...	...	...	...	...	...	51.6	11.7	39.8	...
Palau	29.9	17.9	11.8	0.2	108.0	94.2	13.7	0.1	97.3	84.6	12.6	0.1	113.3	94.3	17.5	1.5
Upper Middle Income	**19.2**	**6.3**	**5.1**	**7.9**	**18.0**	**5.7**	**5.9**	**6.5**	**24.9**	**7.0**	**10.9**	**7.1**	**48.7**	**7.7**	**27.6**	**13.5**
Fiji	11.5	7.1	4.0	0.4	14.6	5.6	8.7	0.4	27.3	6.6	20.5	0.3	39.4	7.7	30.9	0.8
Marshall Islands	26.9	5.4	6.1	15.4	21.3	5.8	3.0	12.6	22.5	7.3	1.3	13.9	58.0	7.6	24.2	26.2
Tonga	4.2	...	...	...	4.2	0.2	1.8	2.2	7.7	0.6	4.0	3.2	8.6	0.7	3.9	4.0
Tuvalu	...	...	...	...	...	...	...	...	...	...	...	...	14.2	1.6	12.6	...
Lower Middle Income	**11.3**	**0.8**	**10.2**	**0.3**	**16.5**	**0.7**	**14.7**	**1.0**	**18.9**	**1.0**	**16.8**	**1.1**	**23.6**	**1.7**	**20.5**	**1.4**
FSM	...	...	...	...	9.2	6.6	2.6	...	7.1	5.3	1.7	...	6.1	4.7	1.4	...
Kiribati	...	...	...	...	9.8	3.8	3.1	2.9	9.4	4.4	3.3	2.8	9.4	2.1	3.9	3.4
Papua New Guinea	0.1	0.1	0.0	0.0	0.2	0.1	0.0	0.0	0.4	0.2	0.0	0.2	1.3	1.0	...	0.3
Samoa	39.6	1.9	37.1	0.6	45.4	2.0	42.5	0.9	45.9	2.3	42.6	1.0	21.8	3.9	16.2	1.7
Solomon Islands	1.4	0.9	0.0	0.5	2.7	0.5	0.0	2.1	3.0	1.0	0.5	1.2	3.0	1.2	1.6	0.2
Vanuatu	4.0	0.4	3.6	0.0	17.6	0.3	16.2	1.1	26.6	0.5	24.2	2.0	47.6	0.5	43.7	3.5
Unweighted Pacific Average	**14.9**	**4.3**	**8.5**	**2.4**	**27.1**	**13.7**	**11.3**	**2.5**	**32.5**	**12.9**	**17.3**	**2.7**	**40.2**	**14.6**	**24.4**	**4.9**

... = no data, 0.0 = value is less than 0.01, FSM = Federated States of Micronesia, LMP = labor market program, SA = social assistance, SI = social insurance, SPI = Social Protection Indicator.

Source: ADB estimates based on consultants' country reports.

Table A9: Gross Domestic Product and Social Protection by Country, 2018

Country	GDP ($ million)	GDP per Capita ($)	Share of Social Protection Expenditures to GDP (%)
Cook Islands	374.44	23,549.64	4.0
Fiji	5,529.86	6,231.58	4.3
FSM	402.00	3,854.78	6.4
Kiribati	202.55	1,766.92	12.0
Nauru	124.03	10,909.58	3.4
Niue	31,097.09	18,462.00	8.4
Palau	285.30	16,304.00	14.1
Papua New Guinea	24,158.76	2,675.99	1.0
Marshall Islands	221.30	4,056.00	11.6
Samoa	823.55	4,150.39	0.0
Solomon Islands	1,536.82	2,202.92	2.2
Tonga	487.83	4,874.36	1.7
Tuvalu	49.53	4,713.93	11.4
Vanuatu	0.91	3,207.02	3.0
Pacific Average			**6.0**

FSM = Federated States of Micronesia, GDP = gross domestic product.

Source: ADB estimates based on consultants' country reports.

Table A10: Social Protection Expenditures as Share to Total Expenditures (%)

Country	Social Insurance	Social Assistance	Labor Market Programs
Cook Islands	13.74	86.26	0.00
Fiji	66.64	31.73	1.63
FSM	84.88	15.12	0.00
Kiribati	33.62	7.94	58.44
Nauru	4.08	95.92	0.00
Palau	87.44	10.51	2.05
Papua New Guinea	98.96	0.00	1.04
Marshall Islands	80.46	8.74	10.81
Samoa	71.48	27.31	1.22
Solomon Islands	98.18	0.13	1.69
Tonga	69.51	26.80	3.69
Tuvalu	34.87	65.13	0.00
Vanuatu	26.29	72.81	0.90
Pacific Average	**59.24**	**34.49**	**6.27**

FSM = Federated States of Micronesia.

Source: ADB estimates based on consultants' country reports.

Table A11: Share of Social Protection Expenditures to Gross Domestic Product by Category, 2018
(%)

Country	Total Social Protection	Social Insurance	Social Assistance	Labor Market Programs
Cook Islands	4.0	0.5	3.4	0.0
Fiji	4.3	2.8	1.4	0.1
FSM	6.4	5.4	1.0	0.0
Kiribati	12.0	4.0	1.0	7.0
Nauru	3.4	0.1	3.2	0.0
Niue	8.4	1.2	7.2	0.0
Palau	14.1	12.4	1.5	0.3
Papua New Guinea	1.0	1.0	0.0	0.0
Marshall Islands	11.6	9.4	1.0	1.3
Samoa	3.3	2.4	0.9	0.0
Solomon Islands	2.2	2.1	0.0	0.0
Tonga	1.7	1.2	0.5	0.1
Tuvalu	11.4	4.0	7.4	0.0
Vanuatu	3.0	0.8	2.2	0.0
Average	**6.2**	**3.4**	**2.2**	**0.6**

FSM = Federated States of Micronesia.

Source: ADB estimates based on consultants' country reports.